NOTHING (EVERYTHING CHANGES

Living with new perspectives

Tsem Tulku Rinpoche

Kechara Media and Publications
2006

ISBN 983-41887-7-3

Published by
Kechara Media and Publications Sdn. Bhd.
37B, 2nd Floor, Jalan SS2/75,
47300 Petaling Jaya, Selangor, Malaysia
Tel: (+603) 7710 4984 Fax: (+603) 7710 3262
Email: kmp@kecharapub.com
Website: www.kecharapub.com

First printing: 2000 copies
Printed by: Percetakan NPK Sdn Bhd

Acknowledgements

The teachings in this book were given at different times and places, which were recorded and subsequently transcribed by Joseph Chan, Andreas Uetz and Jamie Khoo.

We are extremely grateful to our Teacher, His Eminence Tsem Tulku Rinpoche, for giving these teachings and for his guidance at all stages of producing this book. Thank you, Rinpoche.

A big thank you also to Joseph Chan for coordinating the production of this book; 1am Concept for design; Loh Seng Piow for recording the teachings and making them so readily available on DVDs; Sharon Saw and Susan Lim for extensive checking and proofreading.

KMP group of writers

Tsem Tulku Rinpoche

Born of Mongolian-Tibetan heritage, brought up in America and trained by some of Tibet's most prominent Buddhist masters, Tsem Tulku Rinpoche bridges the gap between East and West, bringing the ancient wisdom of Buddhist teachings to our contemporary world.

Drawn to the Dharma since childhood, Rinpoche left America at 19 and was ordained by H.H. the 14th Dalai Lama in India. He studied at Gaden Monastery, one of Tibet's most prestigious universities now located in South India. There he was recognized as a 'Tulku' from an illustrious lineage. His Gurus include H.H. the 14th Dalai Lama, H.H. Kyabje Ling Dorje Chang, H.H. Gaden Tripa (Jampal Zhenphen), H.H. Kyabje Zong Rinpoche, Kensur Lobsang Tharchin Rinpoche (Sera Mey), attained Master Geshe Tsultrim Gyeltsen. He is now based in Malaysia, where he has been teaching for more than 10 years.

Rinpoche is most beloved for the "neon wisdom" he brings to Dharma teachings, locating them in contexts relevant for the modern practitioner and imbuing teachings with humour. He constantly reminds us that we need not compromise who we are to be able to practise Dharma. As a fan of Madonna, Mother Teresa and Versace, Rinpoche teaches us to loosen up and be ourselves, but better!

Under his guidance, the Dharma centre Kechara House was set up in Kuala Lumpur and over the years has expanded to include a publishing house and various Dharma stores. All these have the sole intention of bringing benefit to others and assisting people to find their own spiritual path to happiness.

CONTENTS

Preface

Preface
— ◦ —

One of my friends lives with her father and two little nieces, horrible little monsters that make it a point to wreak as much havoc in the house as possible.

One day, while playing yet another prank on their dear old grandfather, they tested his patience so much he promptly exploded in a rage and began to yell.

The littlest girl, only about four years old, went up to him and pointed out, her nose in the air, "Ah Kong[1], I didn't make you angry. You made yourself angry!" and ran off to cause more trouble.

How completely aggravating but totally true. It's almost surprising that it takes a four-year-old to remind us of this simple truth that most of the time, we make ourselves angry. Things don't turn out the way we want or expect so we throw a fit, get depressed, take it out at everyone around us and in the process, make ourselves unhappy.

A 21st-Century world dictates that the "baddies" are on the outside. Newspapers, movies, stories from our friends thrive on the injustices done by others – good versus bad, baddie verses hero, them versus me. The increasing number of trips to psychiatrists and therapists to puzzle out our depressions almost always link the cause to something that was or is being done to us by someone else – an abusive parent, the husband that left us, an uncompromising, demanding boss.

And then suddenly, in these teachings, Tsem Tulku Rinpoche gives us a shocking new message that we are the biggest perpetrator of our problems. Just like the grandfather, we make ourselves angry – not the husband, the wife, the colleague, the sister, the parent, the rest of the world.

It may seem disheartening at first – after all, it's so much easier pointing fingers at others than to take responsibility for ourselves. It's hard to suddenly get off the soap box and go into a guilt trip for causing our own unhappiness. But there also is the inherent message within these teachings that we're not bad for doing what we do – getting angry, cheating on women, wasting our hard-earned money on ridiculous amounts of alcohol, bad mouthing the people who've hurt us, taking out our disappointments on

▶ [1] Chinese for "Grandfather"

9

everyone else – but that there is another way of living and looking that can bring a profound yet blissful peace of mind.

And all we've needed to do all along is transform part of the way we look at things. We strike at the heart of all our problems and then things really do start to change, without anything actually changing at all…

A note on editing

The following teachings are direct and original transcripts of talks given by H. E. Tsem Tulku Rinpoche, which have been lightly edited for grammar and style.

In almost every teaching, Rinpoche discusses several different topics which tend to overlap and run in a loop. In keeping the flow of the teaching, these topics have not been broken up and edited into separate sections. Instead, for ease of reading, subheadings have been placed at important "breaks" in the teachings, where certain particularly strong messages and themes are highlighted.

Original recordings of these teachings are also available on CD, DVD or can be downloaded online at www.tsemtulku.com. These edited transcripts are not meant to replace the talks themselves and it is highly recommended that the reader complement this book by listening or watching the talks. It gives a much richer experience and understanding of both the teachings and Rinpoche's dynamic approach to Dharma.

~ Jamie Khoo

WHY I MAKE MYSELF UNHAPPY

Why I Make Myself Unhappy

All experiences we have fade into a dream but the activities we do during those experiences do not fade…

…These are my notes that, when I woke up, I wrote down. Everything that you've experienced from the time you were born up until now, many of those things, many, many details you can't remember anymore – you can't. You can't even recall. In fact, when someone tells you something or reminds you about it, you go, "Oh, did that happen?" Or sometimes little bits and memories come back.

Even when we were a little child, things that we threw fits on – we threw our bottles down, we screamed and we hit our mothers and fathers – they were so serious at the time. At that moment it was happening, it was so incredibly serious, but now it's just a distant dream. But us, being the bratty little kids that we were, throwing tantrums and fits are not forgotten. And when we grow up as adults, when we're temperamental and we're difficult and we're angersome, our parents or people who knew us will say, "Oh yeah, they were like that as a child."

So what happens is whatever we do, the experiences that we have fade away, and they go away and they disappear and they don't matter anymore. In fact, by next week you won't even remember we had a Dharma teaching this week. And for some of us what was taught here and explained here by next week is already forgotten. That's not an insult. That's the way our mind works, unfortunately.

The experiences we have, whether it's pleasant or unpleasant, we experience the experience like watching a drama or a play; during a drama or play it's very intense if the actors and actresses are really good. They make you cry, they make you laugh, they make you feel, they make you feel anxiety – you feel real. Why? Because your mind is totally absorbed in that play, totally, but when the play is over, when the show is over, you come back to reality. You know that it was just a play, that it was just actors and actresses.

And sometimes we hear about actors and actresses and what they do – you know, in the bad little gossip magazines. We like them for a few reasons. I like them. I put them near my toilet bowl so when I take my number two I read those. I can't read Dharma books in there so I bring the next best thing – samsara! So I have my little gossip magazines about who's having what liposuction, who broke up with whom, who's with whom, who's suspected of this and all that stuff, you know, and I put it next to my toilet and I read it when I'm taking my number two.

We like those and we read those and we feel interested because one of the reasons is that when we see these actors and actresses on the screen, they portray a very good person, a wonderful person, or a very rotten, evil person. They portray a certain kind of character and we kind of identify them with that. So when we read these magazines and they don't match the character, we find it interesting.

For example, you may see an actress play the part of a nun where she is really holy and blah, blah, blah like Audrey Hepburn in that nun story. And when she's so wonderful and holy, fabulous and everything and then you read in the magazine she's divorced four times, you're like, "What kind of nun is that?!" And you find it interesting. Why? Because it doesn't match their character. So we like that. That's something subconscious in all of us, and we're like, "Oh, they can do that and they can do this and it's fun."

In any case, similarly, things that happen to us, good and bad, are like a play or a show. Think about it. No matter how much intensity we put into the experience, the experience will pass, what happens will pass. And the person we had the good and bad experience with will pass and go away, and they fade into a dream. Think about relationships and friends and people you've known ten years ago, five years ago, four years ago, a year ago. Some you can't even remember. Some you don't want to remember.

They fade, and even the people we have relationships with now and in the future will be memories, sometimes not even memories. But the actions we do with them do not become memories. What we do with people and the experiences do not become memories.

For example, when we're riding in traffic and someone cuts us off and we immediately aggressively chase after them, the chasing will be done, but the action of anger and chasing them and wanting to get them and scare them and get them back and teach them a lesson doesn't go away. Why? We reinforce our anger, we experience the anger and we feel familiar with it. And when there are no immediate repercussions, we engage in it again and again and again, until it becomes something very serious.

Similarly, if we have a negative experience with someone, a negative experience, once it's over, that person is gone. Maybe we don't talk to them ever again. The experience we had with that person is gone, but the action we've done with that person is not gone. Whatever we've said and done that is hurtful and damaging to the other person equates into karma, and that karma remains and that karma goes on.

And the horrible part about that karma is that it multiplies daily. And the next horrible thing about karma is that it comes back to us. So whatever we do with the person – whether it's our parents, whether it's our girlfriends and boyfriends, whether it's friends, whether it's social people, whether it's the fancy of the moment – it will pass. And when it passes, we can't even remember any more. But unfortunately the action stays.

And if you don't believe in karma it's okay also; I'm not here to force it down your throats. But if you don't believe in karma you can believe in this: the action stays because you reinforce your action. Let's say we're very attached to a relationship and we put all our energy into a relationship. It fades, it goes away, and all the energy and time that we put into our relationship is gone. It's totally gone and if we try to recapture or get it back it'll be worse than before. It will never be like before. The karma for it is gone.

Now if we have a good relationship and then we end it; and then we want another good relationship, we end it; then we have this power of ending relationships or we have the power of not wanting relationships. What happens is a time will come when our karma builds up and someone will do it back to us. And we won't be able to take it. If we don't have Dharma, if we don't have a good psychological background, we won't be able to take it. We may go off the deep end, commit suicide, do something violent, hurt, get revenge – we can do a lot of things. So even so-called "good" relationship experiences end up bad because they reinforce something that's not real.

We focus on relationships, people, money, friends and reputation as the outlet for happiness, but eventually we will have to face ourselves

We cannot get happiness from a relationship. We cannot get happiness from money. We cannot get it from people, from outside things. Why? Because number one, they don't last. Number two, these outer things are not permanent. Number three, the foundation that these outer things (such as money, reputation, family, friends) sit on is very fragile. Like when the Tsunami hit, over 200,000 people died, just in one or two hours. It's very fragile, it goes away.

Although this building is very solid, it will go away. Although we think our bodies are very solid, it will go away, it will disintegrate. So when we focus on relationships and people and money and friends and reputation, cars and entertainment as the outlet for happiness, or hiding behind something because we're not happy, eventually we will have to face ourselves. And when we face ourselves, you know what's the horrible part? That when the merit and the karma for those things run out, perhaps we cannot overcome it. And that's why people do extreme things.

When the experience is over, what we have done creates a reputation for us that even before the actual results come, people form preconceived ideas of who we are, what we are and how they think we are. True or not doesn't matter. People experience us as we experience them.

If you don't believe in karma – because I always teach on two levels; I share on two levels – if you don't believe in karma, it's okay also because Buddha can be used as a psychology that helps. He's the great psychologist. He is a Buddha, definitely, but he can be used on different levels in a positive way. That's what he wants. Whatever experience we have, whether it's positive or negative, how we act during that experience and how we act immediately after that experience and how we act in relation to what happened creates even more karma.

But on a normal worldly psychological level, whatever experience we have and the way we act and talk and show our face and show our body language at that time, during that experience, people will hear, people will see, and that will formulate their preconceived notions about us.

So, if normally you're sloppy, you are unaware, you forget things, if normally you don't pay attention, you're not alert; if normally you're angersome, you react back negatively; if normally you're irresponsible, if normally you're very responsible; if normally you're very kind, you're very gentle; if normally you're very skilful, if normally you're very enthusiastic to help; if normally you're very lazy and you hide and you say things and you don't fulfil your commitments or you push or you hide behind your tears – if normally you are like that and you do these things for a long time, that formulates the conceived idea about you and others, and that conception of you creates your reputation.

And that reputation of you, true or false, creates more conceptions about you from others and that conception about us is what hurts us, because we always complain, "I'm misunderstood. People don't understand me." And we spend a lot of time in our speech explaining ourselves to others, talking about ourselves to others, justifying ourselves to others and explaining and talking. But when we look at ourselves deeply we have no results.

We have no results but we're very eloquent in explaining why. And we spend our time on why we didn't get it and we spend our time explaining and telling, and then most of us – those people who explain – usually have not accomplished anything in our lives but we can explain why.

So my question is if you can explain why, why don't you have an answer to do something to change it? Since you know why, you must also know an antidote. So if you don't know an antidote, two ways: find one in the Buddha or in a friend that has wisdom, but don't stick in your narrow way of thinking and view and action because it gets you nowhere. Nowhere, no success.

If we have a bad relationship with our father and our mother, if we have a bad relationship with our wife and our husband, if we have a bad relationship with our friends or with people we meet and we're misunderstood, instead of always explaining, we need to understand that we created that reputation about ourselves directly or indirectly.

And even in this life, if you think yourself very good and you didn't do much, in your ignorance, in your darkness, you think you didn't do much and that people just think like that and they accuse you – that also comes from a cause. Because however you are, maybe you're not consciously doing it but you're subconsciously doing it on a conscious level without knowing it.

People can misunderstand you by the way you do things but should we spend the rest of our lives explaining about how good we are? Or do we live in a world with a lot of sentient beings and we need to accommodate because we're social beings? Even in this life if you didn't do much, perhaps the habituation came from a previous life.

It's very big these days, past-life regression therapy in America. Very, very big. They don't even believe in Buddhism and they do that because what Buddha teaches us is true. It's not based on some religious dogma, it's true. We do have past lives, we do.

Many of the major religions in the world accepted that at one point or another, but it was banned at one point or another. Why do I point out religion? Because you get very wise people from religious practice. Because they settle their minds and they're able to reach higher states of meditation where they can hear, see or contact deeper levels of consciousness. In all religions. That's why all religious people in any religion can have religious experiences, see Mother Mary, see Tara, whatever.

They can because once they reach a certain level of the mind, relaxing through whatever meditation, they open up the subconscious, they open up deeper, they open up past life memories. And if we can remember things from this life, why can't we remember things from previous lives? It's only a matter of exercising that power of concentration.

Transformation today will create new ideas about us tomorrow

If we have a difficulty with certain people in our lives or certain situations or if we're not doing anything and we are accused and people say things about us, or people have a certain view about us, we have to ask ourselves what did we do to create that misconception?

If people think we're lazy, if people think we shirk responsibility, have we done that? If we have, we remain silent and change. If we haven't, instead of trying to justify what we've done, we should realise by the power of cause and effect that we have created this in previous lives. That habituation started somewhere, whether a year ago, two years ago, three years ago or a lifetime ago or ten lifetimes ago. It started somewhere.

So people's preconceptions about us come from the way we have reacted in the past to experiences. And the way we react to experiences and how we talk and how we do things are the notions, reputation, conceptions that people put on us. And then even people who didn't meet us, they'll spread your reputation out, and add things to it, and even increase what they say about you.

So we have two ways: we can spend the rest of our lives defending ourselves and putting all our energy into telling people how right we are and how we're misunderstood but not put our energy into transforming ourselves. We only have a certain amount of energy and a certain amount of time. So if we put all our energy and time into explaining and justifying, then by the end, yeah, we justified ourselves but we have no result. If we're into material things, we have no car, we have no apartment, we have no partner, we have no friends, everybody has abandoned us - we're alone. Even the people who try to help us, we alienate them. This is on a worldly level.

On a spiritual level, when you die, maybe you get a good life, maybe not. Think! So if we have so limited an amount of energy and time, wouldn't it be better to put this into transforming ourselves, so that the preconceived ideas about us will slowly crumble away? It won't be as fast as if we talked directly but it will be more effective and longer lasting.

And how do we transform ourselves now? It's by learning the Dharma. Learning the Dharma, contemplating, listening to Dharma teachings, meditating. Contemplating and putting that into our lives and creating a transformation. And that transformation today will create the new ideas about us tomorrow.

I had a lot of difficult experiences as a child. A lot of horrible experiences; physical and mental. Lots and lots of horrible physical abuse and mental abuse as a child. I choose to use those experiences to not create a further reputation for myself. I will not take the anger towards me and put that anger towards others and to damage others but I choose to take that anger to realise that I did something in a previous life to get that. Therefore, I accept it.

By accepting, letting go and forgiving, I purify that karma. It's done. That karma is used up. I can't use it any more. It's like a paper cup or a paper plate; once I've used it I can't let the other person use it again. It's done. But if I harp on it, I focus on it, I use it again and I do it again and I think about it and I do negative things in relation to it or I justify my actions by saying that it came from the fact that I was hurt and abused, no one, at the end, will accept that any more. In the beginning, for one or two sessions, but not on a continual basis.

But people who don't want to take courage in doing something more and take action and responsibility, they will justify their actions from previous actions done to them. "My husband was bad to me." "My wife was bad to me." "My husband cheated on me." "My wife lied to me." "My mother was bad to me." "My father was a womaniser." They go on and on and on and use that continually as an excuse for their state of being now.

Yes, maybe those were contributing factors, I agree, but right now what is contributing to your downfall? *Right now* what is contributing to your lack of knowledge and your justifications? *What is it that you're doing now*? So if those experiences can lead to what you are now, your experiences now can lead to what you will be tomorrow.

So, in the past you may have had a rotten husband that cheated on you, that lied to you, and, therefore, you're out in the cold and you have to work like a slave; or in the past you had rotten parents that abused you and beat you and did a lot of bad things to you, and you're out in the cold now and you didn't get an education and you've had a difficult time. Yes, that's how you are now and it happened. Accepted, on a worldly level.

But what about right now? You can't live the rest of your life based on what happened to you and use that continuously. You can't because that is your grasping and holding on to a projection, to something that happened to you and not letting go. And you're still creating karma from that event.

For example, my parents were very against me practising Buddhism. They wanted me to go to college, they wanted me to get married, I already had the girl settled, because that's their way. Her name was Pemba, a very nice girl. They wanted me to get into education and I was threatened. My father told me if I marry a black girl, he will hang me. He said he meant it. "No Jews, no blacks, white girls can play with them and drop them off, but you marry a yellow girl.

Best is your own race, if not, Chinese, Japanese, can." That was his rule. Good or bad I'm not trying to tell you.

And they wanted me to go to college; they didn't want me to go to Dharma. They used to call up and say nasty things to my teacher, spread rumours about my teacher saying he was having sex with everybody, with all the females in the neighbourhood. Some people believed, ninety per cent didn't. It didn't matter. I didn't care.

They did that, and if my mother was successful in stopping me from doing the Dharma, we wouldn't be here today. And my mother would have collected incredible negative karma. Because if I was to be a Dharma teacher and I am to touch a thousand people in my life, she would have stopped me from touching one thousand people, which is much more than education; because if I get an education, if I have a degree, what's to guarantee me that I'll be successful, what's to guarantee me I'll be a good person? Okay, I'll work a job, struggle and get some money. What's to guarantee I'll even live long enough to do all that? What's to guarantee my mother will live long enough to do that?

But I respect her and I pray for her and make offerings for her because that's all she knew, that was her level of practice. That was her level of person. So, her best and my father's best was that. They couldn't go any higher. But with respect to them, I knew more. I understood more. I knew what I had to do. I hate this word but I had a "calling". It was very deep.

So I resisted, I fought, I ran away. I ran away from my parents a lot, and I hurt my stepmother and stepfather tremendously because I wanted to do the Dharma. But I took courage, because I didn't do it to hurt them. I did it because I knew what I needed to do. So, when we stop people from doing Dharma, if it's real, it's genuine, it's incredible karma.

When I was very young, I was told by my nanny that at the age of seven months, they already recognised me as a reincarnation, they've already put the golden robes on me, literally. But my mother refused. My real mother at that time refused for me to be enthroned. She told the monks who came to take me to the monasteries, "If he's a real Rinpoche, when he grows up he'll find his way. If I put him in now, I don't know if he'll go right or wrong. Don't know if what you guys are saying is right or wrong. But when he grows up, he'll go the right way." I was angry at that time, when I was younger when I heard this. But now I understand.

My point is this: whatever happens to us, right now, yes, it's based on something that happened in the past. But if we keep basing what we do now, tomorrow, the next day, the next week, the next year on what's happened in the past we just keep living the way we are and go worse, because a time comes when age comes, when our metabolism slows down and when the energy and zest of youth goes away, it's very difficult. And if we have the energy and zest of youth it's not a big deal either, because most youths while their times away at activities that destroy themselves eventually, emotionally.

So, what we experienced in the past, we base it on that experience and we keep holding on to it – "this person was bad," "this situation was bad," "I was born poor," "I lived in the streets," "I slept outside," "I was beaten," "someone cheated me" – and we hold on to that and we live that and when we do everything in relation to that, we lose on a worldly level.

And, everybody we wish to help and every prayer that we say that we wish to benefit all sentient beings as we pray in Buddhism is a farce, is a lie, is not true and we're fooling ourselves. Why? If we can't even let go of something that happened that we actually created – maybe we were a bitchy wife, maybe we were a demanding husband, maybe we were a nasty person that contributed to this person doing things to us – if we keep holding on to what happened and basing on those experiences and doing actions based on those experiences, we lose. Why? If we were at fault for what happened, we are reinforcing that fault and we'll do it again and again and again to the new people we meet.

If we are not at fault, we are creating the fault because when we hold on to it and we act out of it, we create more karma to, in fact, have it happen again. Because, I may say Chia, he's my older brother and he was very mean to me when I was young. He used to beat me, he used to take my food away, take my toys and he did that for years. When I grow up I become a successful business guy and I get him back. He's working as a grease monkey somewhere, fixing cars and I get him back. When he comes to ask for money I make him kowtow and kiss my ass. *I get him back.* You see, what he did to me is over but I do it to him because I'm holding on to experience and I create more and more and more karma.

Everything is based on you changing your reputation

For people who say, "I'm lazy," "Oh, I'm not aware," "Oh, I'm attached," "Oh, I have desire," "That's the way I am but I'm working on it" – B.S.! In fact that itself is an attachment and a lame excuse for you to continue what you're doing to create yourself the next time. When you actually tell people, "I'm full of desire," "I'm lazy," "I have bad speech," "I'm not aware," "I can't do this, I can't do that", you are reinforcing it because you are using that as an excuse not to become better.

That is called attachment based on wrong projection that comes from the deepest suffering – ignorance. The main factor for us to stay in samsara is when we reinforce it over and over: "I can't, I won't, I don't, I don't have time, I can't, I just can't, it's hard, I'll try."

You know what's the worst word that puts you down? When you say, "I will try." It's very bad because you give yourself "fifty-fifty" that you won't. And if you know yourself, if you have a reputation of not fulfilling your commitments and not doing what you're supposed to do and disappointing a lot of people; if you are that type of person, disappointing people, letting people down, letting your anger take over, getting revenge, being lazy, not fulfilling your commitments; if you're that type of person, when you say "I will try", you allow yourself to fail.

Some of you may think, "Oh, but that's my way of not letting people down." You're already letting them down, because you already have the reputation of being that way! So what you need to say is, "I will" and do it. Whatever reputation was made in the past can be changed now for the future. So if you were this way, if you were orange in the past, you can be red in the future. If you are red today you can be green the next day. Everything is based on you changing your reputation.

So, therefore, whatever you were, doesn't have to be the same tomorrow. Whatever you are now doesn't have to remain. Whatever you want to be can happen now. Why? Because you put in what you want to be. You become what you put your energy towards. So, if you are self-deprecating and you say you cannot or you put yourself down by not doing because you base it on a past experience, then you are a very attached person. If you are a very attached person in Dharma, it's very hard to improve and become better.

And the best way to let go of that attachment, the best remedy is realising you are attached, listening to Dharma teachings on removal of attachment, collecting merit and doing practices to cut out that attachment. Because if it's attachment, it brings unhappiness; if it's attachment-based, it brings disharmony; if it's attachment-based, no matter how good things are now, no matter how good your motivation supposedly is, it will bring about unhappiness.

The law in samsara is everything is impermanent and will end. You need to remember that truth and you need to keep that in your mind. So long as we understand that truth, everything becomes easier. It's not something that makes you depressed, it is something that actually helps you to become better.

Our upbringing, our culture, our background and what we expect... is false

We need to let go of conventions, projections, cultures, upbringing, expectations of experiences. That will help us let go. We will feel less at a loss. We'll feel less loss, and we'll find a purpose in our lives. I repeat: due to past experiences we hold on to conventions.

If we are Chinese, at Chinese New Year's, everything must be red or we won't have fortune. But that means everybody who doesn't have red on Chinese New Year's must be a failure. And then we get attached to that. What I'm saying here is I'm not putting down Chinese culture and five thousand years of rich Chinese heritage. What I'm saying is if it suits everybody to have red, have red! If you go home to your family in Penang or Ipoh or Telok Intan or Grik or Kelantan or Tibet, and they want red and it makes them happy, put red. But if you go to another place and you have to have red and they don't want red and then a big argument ensues, it's not a happy "Gong Xi Fa Chai" is it?

What I'm saying is that is convention. Those are things created by humans who don't have wisdom, which says we need to do things in a certain way, otherwise good fortune or good things won't come. Celebrate Chinese New Year, wear red, have red houses, everything red. Be red! Hang out in Jalan Alor [1], red! No problem! But, if you're in a place that doesn't understand, know

▶ [1] A red light district in Kuala Lumpur.

that you don't have to have that and force it down people, to say, "I have to have it." Holding culture, holding convention can be beneficial but if we do it wrong, it could be evil. It could hurt people.

Similarly, projections: how we expect a situation to be, how we expect a person to be. Most of us – and contemplate deeply please – most of us suffer because our projections are not fulfilled. Most of us. We have a projection of how a certain situation must be, we have a projection of how people should be, we have a certain projection of how we must do certain things.

And when we do it and that projection doesn't happen and it doesn't materialise as we have projected, we become angry. Why? Because our upbringing, our culture, our background and what we expect is *false*. Then we create sufferings for other people and other situations. Why? Other people don't have the same upbringing as us, other people don't have the same values and thinking and culture and background as us. How can everybody be exactly as us?

And we have a false expectation of others. When we plant that false expectations on others, and they don't meet up to it, we get into a cat fight. We scold or we show a black face or we say nasty things. We create more sufferings for them and us. And if you don't believe in karma and religion and Buddha, no problem, but you can believe in humanity.

You don't create harmony and happiness by your projections. You don't create harmony and happiness when you actually do that to other people. Because if you don't believe in the next life, no problem. *Believe in this life*. Believe that if you do that, that's not right.

And that's the beauty of Dharma and Dharma teachings. It's that it can be applied to your life and it can benefit your life *now*. People who take time to listen to Dharma, people who make time for Dharma, people who do that have their priorities correct. I'll tell you why. You're not a religious fanatic. Whatever we do, whatever we put time toward is to bring some kind of benefit to us. What's more beneficial than learning the most ultimate way of transforming our mind to bring benefit to others?

So, if we don't have any methods that are ultimate, we don't make time to learn, we don't make time for it, we don't have our priorities straight, then whatever we do will only be limited and stunted, and we cannot reach our full potential. Why? No matter how smart and good we are, there's someone better and smarter, for example, Buddha. So it's very important how we act, how we talk, how we present ourselves.

People can be beaten and react positively. People can be beaten and react negatively

How we live is due to experiences or dreams – dreams as in what we wanted to be, what we wanted to do or hopes we had earlier in life or even in a previous life. So sometimes it's hard to understand, but let go and know it doesn't affect us anymore. Change now. We react now to what has happened. So changing in Dharma, with Dharma, by Dharma creates new attitudes to experience now and in the future. So we don't create more negative reputation for ourselves, perpetuating negatively about ourselves and others and reaffirming our further negative actions.

Meaning what? However we're acting now, however we react to people now, whatever we're doing to other people now is based on experiences we had in the past, and based on our hopes and dreams of the past. Based on that – whether they're false or real – based on that.

So, if we're creating a lot of negative karma, it's due to the experiences we had in the past. But not even that; if we go deeper, it's due to the *reactions* we have to the experiences in the past. People can be beaten and react positively. People can be beaten and react negatively.

People, deep Dharma practitioners who were beaten, they move on; they say, "I purified my karma. I'll avoid that, it's okay. I forgive the person" and they don't create more harm. People who don't, they probably get revenge, they go kill, they get angry and they become angersome people and they do more hurt to other people. They maybe kill other people or beat other people. The experience is there, and I don't deny that. Buddhism doesn't deny that. I don't deny the experience. What I deny is how we react to the experience, what we do in conjunction to that experience. And not just immediately after that experience but next year, next year, next year, next year, even up until now.

What happened to us in the past is what we are now; but what will happen to us in the future depends on what we *do* now. And we can change what will happen only by seeking higher wisdom to deal with it. One higher wisdom is Buddha's Dharma, and that will have effect. But if we continuously don't put effort toward that, then what is happening to us now, due to the reactions we had to experiences in the past, will continue until we die. And unfortunately, continue into our future lives.

So, if you are a great meditator in this life, you'll be one in your next life – greater. If you had practised Dharma very deeply in your previous life, in this life, from a very young age you'll seek the Dharma. If in your previous life you sought after money, food, drugs and sex, you will seek that now. If in your previous life, you were always seeking financial security, some kind of praise and beauty and name and fame, you will seek that now.

And unfortunately for people who seek things that are wrong, you won't go to hell. *You create* hell. Because in your seeking of it, you will not attain it. And when you have attained so-called "what you want" that is based on attachment, you will create more negative karma for it to be taken away.

How beautiful you are, you will not be beautiful one day; how rich you are, it will be taken away at the time of death

…That's true, whether you want to believe in Dharma or not. How beautiful you are, you will not be beautiful one day. How healthy you are, you will not be healthy. How young you are, you will not be young. How rich you are, one day it will be taken away, lost, given away, for you leave it at the time of death. How many children you have, how attached you are to your children, one day they will leave the flock. If you've set them the right way, wonderful; if you didn't set them the right way, they may make it, they may not make it. Ultimately, you have to let go.

If you have wonderful parents that take care of you, give you money, give you love, give you cars, food, house, everything that you want, they will be gone. And don't think that, "Oh, when they're gone I'll have a big inheritance," because if you don't have the merit to have it; if you don't have the luck to have it, when your parents are gone, they take their luck with them.

So, when their luck is gone, you don't have luck anymore. You will go down. So, a lot of kids, after their parents die, go down. A lot, I've seen it. Why? Because this is my job-to interview people, to see people, to talk to people. I've met thousands, all levels, all cultures, this is my job.

I've met a lot of kids who come from extremely wealthy families. Once their parents are gone, the kids fall – boom! They can't even get a job, they work somewhere cutting paper. And I'm not putting anyone down. Why? Because when they don't have the luck but they live with someone who has the luck, they get something.

For example, if you don't smell good but you stand next to someone that smells good, you smell their smell (they can smell your smell too...). Okay, so when you're around some one who smells good (they smell really good because they put on Christian Dior, they put on Passion or whatever and they drank the whole bottle, you know what I mean!) and someone comes near, they think, "Oh, you all smell so good." But the minute that person goes away, they smell you and they go, "Oh, you smell... interesting," correct?

Similarly, if your parents are very wealthy and you are there, everybody looks at you, "Oh you guys are so lucky. What, you're all so rich, got everything." If your parents drop dead, they go away, they are finished, they are no more, suddenly you are smelly. If you don't have the luck to have the wealth, you won't get a dime. I promise you! If I am wrong, Buddha is wrong. I am not backing up what I say with the Buddha. I am telling you the truth about karma.

So if you are riding high now and you are having a great time and you are just living life and you are just going along enjoying yourself and letting daddy and mommy give you everything (I wish I had one like that but I don't!) and you are just going along, if they go off, if they pass away, they may have *10 billion dollars* to give you... they may have 10 billion dollars but if you don't have the luck to have it – maybe something goes wrong in the courts, with relatives, someone – you can't get it. I promise you. So you better get your act together now, that's what I always tell myself.

Similarly, that is for everything in life. If that person is very powerful and they smell good, once they are gone your smell comes out because you go along with your karma. You think about that. Does that make sense? Is that logical?

Even what I am telling you now is Dharma talk. Even some of you who have taken the time to come listen to Dharma for one or two hours, when you leave here you get more knowledge; that is what you get. That is what you do for yourself. I don't charge you. There is no entrance fee.

I don't get anything from you by teaching you Dharma. There is no benefit for me. In fact I take time away from watching movies. I brought some new movies yesterday. I am dying to go home and watch it, because I am not "attached"... so I take time away from my personal life to come here to share knowledge with you that I have taken twenty years to learn, through a lot of sacrifice. (I lived in a little house in India. Later it was a big house but anyway, in the beginning it was a little hut, living under my teachers).

So when you leave here after two hours, you did something for yourself. You get knowledge that is over 2,500 years old from the Buddha. You win. So, if you make the effort, you stay awake, you put yourself here and you sit and you listen, you win.

If you are having a great life now because your parents have given it to you, your company is giving it to you, your girlfriend is giving it to you, your wife is giving it to you, your husband is giving it to you, your boyfriend is giving it to you, your lover is giving it to you; whatever, however you are getting it - you have to make sure that when they are gone, you have the luck to continue that way of life. Because if you don't, *pfff*!... no joke.

So don't be riding high now. And some of us who are riding high now without any personal effort, let me tell you something. According to Kensur Jhampa Yeshe Rinpoche[2], it is the speedy way of burning up your merit and not having anything later. Meaning, I may live with my father and he takes care of everything and I don't take responsibility for myself in any way, shape or form; and I just live the good life and I just go popping along here and there and I don't do anything, I don't take advantage of that.

But, for example, even if I am being taken care of and I go for education, I improve myself, I work harder, I establish myself and I do something with my life even though I am being sheltered by my father or my uncle, my company, my friend, whatever. I am still being sheltered by them but even if I fall, I can make sure that when they are gone, I am making it on my own merits, religiously and worldly. Whereas if they are sheltering me now and

▶ 2 Kensur Jhampa Yeshe Rinpoche was one of Tsem Rinpoche's Gurus when he studied in Gaden Monastery and is a very prominent Buddhist master and teacher.

29

I don't take care of myself and I don't do something, when their shelter is gone, I will fall.

And what Kensur Jhampa Yeshe Rinpoche says is that, in fact, that type of person who uses their opportunity not for improving themselves but for just enjoying and laying around, they use up their merit faster and quicker so that when this umbrella or this parent or this person is gone, they will fall even heavier.

And I have seen that in my own family with my own brothers. One of them died of cancer just last year. 42, 43. Why? My father is very wealthy in Taiwan. I don't get anything because I am from a different mother. My brothers are very good looking. Very handsome. Very tall. They are in all the sex-gossip magazines. They send it to me to see which actress they are sleeping with in Taiwan. Not that I care, I don't know why they send that to me... Some of you have seen the magazines my brother sent to me, that he slept with this girl, and he is the Dalai Lama's best friend.

Anyway, one of them has got apartments and houses from my father and he died of cancer because he over-drank and over-smoked and over-partied. He never worked one day in his life. He lived off the salary he got from renting the apartments my father gave him. And he literally died from a good life, last year. Many of you know that.

My sister took land from my father and got US$3 or 4 million out of it and just disappeared to another part of Taiwan and never contacted him again. My other brother is now living under the umbrella of my father. My father has throat cancer, but he is okay now, in remission.

My point is, when my father's umbrella is gone, they will suffer tremendously. Because when we live under someone's luck and merits, and we live under someone's money and fortune and good luck, no matter how close they are to us, when they are gone, we may not get it. And you know what is sad? The people and friends around us who are after that, they will disappear very fast, because that is what happened to my brothers. I am not telling you from a Dharma book, I am not telling you from what I have read. I am telling you from my own experience and it matches what Buddha says.

So, don't think that I had a good life, that I have been living in a golden palanquin in the Potala Palace in Tibet. No! I was living on the streets of L.A., hustling. No, I didn't have the good life.

So, if we are going to live and be the way we are now, please enjoy what you have, but at the same time work for your future, whether you want to do it from a Dharma base, karma, or you want to do it from a self-preservation base – do it. Because what you have now is based on the past, but the past cannot always become the future, and then you may use your merits up very fast.

And may I tell you very honestly and directly without any negativity at all? It is that when I woke up I thought about all this. Must be the crowd coming. I didn't know who is coming. But I write all this down already before I came. So, if anyone in the audience thinks I am pin-pointing you, I am not.
I have written this down before I came and I highlighted the ones in red that are very important and it is just that I am almost done. So, I don't know who is coming but with me it is very strange because depending on the crowd, it depends on what I want to talk about. So I get an inspiration. I know what I want to say and I know what I want to do. So I write everything down, I come and just talk.

Questions and Answers

Q: If I see something's wrong, how do I "back-track" it?

A: Oh, you have already back-tracked it. You know why? She asks if you have done something in accordance with an experience in the past and you realise that what you have done is wrong, what you do now? You have already done something. Because you realised it's wrong and then you contemplate on the time you wasted by focusing on that and the years or the months or days or whatever you wasted by doing that. You contemplate again and again and you think about it.

You don't have to sit there like, "Ommmm." You can just sit there, have a banana and a coffee, have a ciggie butt and think about it. Yes. Because why? Thinking about it again and again is a type of meditation. There are two types. That type is called analytical meditation. It helps you to change your mind and habits. Why? You meditate to the point where you are so disgusted with yourself about that, that you transform.

If someone gives you something to eat and it's actually poisoned, it creates cancer and you didn't know, but you are addicted to it. Wouldn't you give it up eventually once you know? It might take you time because of your addiction, right? But knowing is already there. So when you know that, that's very good. When you know that, it is not even the first step; it's like the fifth step up to the tenth step.

So what you do is you contemplate on what happened, you contemplate on how you reacted, how it affected people, how much time you wasted, what you could have done instead. And then, if you can, you add Dharma knowledge to it to see an alternative and do an alternative because that's what you are now, from that. But what you're going to be tomorrow is what you are doing now.

So, even the two, three hours you sat here listening to Dharma, I am sure you got knowledge. This knowledge you apply and I am sure some of the things you do are going to be different than before you attended this course. Why? Because it's knowledge. And we are intelligent.

Along with that we do preliminary practices and practices. We get more knowledge, because the more knowledge we get, the better we can root out what we have done and how we reacted. How to root it out? Now you need to get the method, and the method is Dharma.

NOTHING CHANGES...

Nothing Changes...

Everything changes and at the same time nothing changes

Everything changes, and at the same time, nothing changes. What's wonderful about Buddha's teachings is that everything changes. Everything: how we perceive people, how we react to people, how we talk, our emotions, our happiness, our anger, our delusions, our jealousies, our successes, our motivations, our enthusiasms, everything completely changes, and yet nothing changes.

Why is that? Because spiritual practice is basically a change of attitude. So people who feel tired of spiritual practice, people who feel unenthusiastic towards spiritual practice, people who feel lazy towards spiritual practice: what happens is that, most of these types of people don't find a lot of meaning in their life. They don't have meaning in their life, not because their life doesn't have meaning; they don't give their life meaning.

So when we want to give our life meaning, as I have said many, many times in the past, it is not a matter of getting outer needs and wealth, it's not a matter of getting outer necessities, it's not a matter of any of that. Nothing, nothing at all. It has nothing to do with outer wealth and outer betterment.

If it had to do with outer betterment, and inner betterment – inner betterment on just a very gross level – then we will see drastic changes in our lives. So we can see that we usually chase – we chase after one thing after another thing after another thing after another thing, and we just chase and chase and we pursue and we call those "goals." And in the process of chasing for goals, we feel happier. Once we get it, we want another goal, we want to change goals, we want a higher goal, we want a better goal, we want a different goal.

And the whole life is chasing after goals, and so in the process of chasing goals, we lose our time, we lose our youth, we lose our friends, sometimes we lose our partners, sometimes we lose people that are close to us. Sometimes we lose things that really, really matter in our lives.

So when we chase after these goals, we have to understand that the goals that we chase after have to be legitimate, that they do bring about some kind of stable, unchanging – and this is the key word – *unchanging* happiness. So what happens is in spiritual practice it has everything to do with everything about you changing, and the beauty of it is nothing changes! Why? In spiritual practice, as you do more and more spiritual practice – real spiritual practice, transformative spiritual practice – you will see your mind become light, you will see your mind become very happy, very bright. And you will see that you accept things, even in the few months that you are in the Dharma (in this case, this spiritual practice). Even after a few days, for some people, few days, few weeks, you see your mind expanding.

For example, things that you normally would not have been able to *tahan*[1] , to take, to forebear, you are able to forebear now. Things that you thought, "Oh my God, I will never be able to do that, I will never want to do that, I will never want to be… that, this, this," whatever, and you have a projection – even one week in the Dharma, when you listen to it, with your heart, with your intelligence, you say "I can bear it."

And what does that indicate to you? When we open our hearts to the Dharma, and we apply it, things that we were not able to do before, we are able to do; things that we found unbearable, we are able to bear.

And, what's the big deal about that? You may think, "Well, I don't want to bear a lot of things." It's not that. When you are cushioned, and your life is easy, and you have things taken care for you, of course it's very easy. But are we sure that it will always be like that? Are we sure?

And even if physically we are cushioned, how about mentally? How about mentally? *Are we cushioned*? Because physically things may not change, but mentally in relationships with people, in finances, in stability, in jobs, in friendships, does it remain stable? If it doesn't remain stable, outwardly we may have a big house and a big car, and everything is nice, and we're very cushioned – we have enough to eat, everything is comfortable, everything is nice – but inwardly are we cushioned?

Inwardly if we're not cushioned, and we're not ready, the minute someone leaves us, the whole world falls apart, our whole world falls apart, our whole reality falls apart. The minute we lose some money, our whole reality falls

▶ [1] Malay/ Malaysian slang for "to bear, to tolerate."

apart. The minute someone says something to us that we don't like, our reality falls apart. The minute someone shows us a black face, or an unpleasant word, our reality falls apart.

And when our reality falls apart, we affect everybody around us: the way we act, the way we talk, the way we react, we hurt everybody and we damage. And sometimes the damage we do to people around us takes a long time to recover or it never recovers.

How we look at things changes everything around us

So when we do spiritual practice, it changes our minds. How does it change our minds? It isn't that you pray more, it isn't that you meditate more, it isn't that you read more. It is a change of attitude, a change of perspective, and how we look at things. And how we look at things changes everything around us, and at the same time, the beauty of it is nothing changes. Nothing at all. *Nothing.*

Why? We remain as we are, our identity. Male, female, Malaysian, foreigner, you like to eat this food, you like to go to sleep at this time, you like to wear these kind of clothes, you like this kind of fashion. You see, none of that changes, but your whole perspective and approach to it completely changes.

Maybe 20 years ago, we were dressed and looked, and did our hair in a way that "dressed to kill," dressed to seduce, dressed to get, dressed to conquer. But now maybe we are still "dressing to kill", but it's not to conquer or to seduce, maybe now it's to invite, or maybe it is to impress people, or maybe it's to accomplish something.

For example, we could have gone dressed before to look for nice girls in a club. Now we dress so that we can get a good job so that we can support our families. So dressing is the same, and the whole process of washing and grooming and shampoos and soap and water and toweling and cologne and perfume is all exactly the same. The whole process is the same. Nothing changes yet what changes is the *motivation* and the object. So spiritual practice is the transformation of our perspective and how we look at things. That is spiritual practice.

And hence the mantras are very powerful, because the mantras are specific words spoken by Lord Buddha's holy mouth himself, which gather the energies in our bodies and the winds to help us, to bring us to the state of perspective that we can change our minds easier.

And there are specific meditation postures, specific mudras, specific exercises, wind, breath, body and mind that the Buddha has designed for our particular type of people in this world, that help us to achieve that state of mind which is a change of perspective. And that's what the mantras are all about, and that's what the sadhanas are all about, and that's what the meditations are all about. Hence the meditational books, the Dharma books and the study of the Dharma.

The study of the Dharma is not Dharma, praying is not Dharma, altars and making offerings is not Dharma, hanging around a holy Guru is not Dharma, not hanging around a holy Guru is not Dharma, having a great centre is not Dharma. What is Dharma? It's the complete turnabout of our attitude and the way we see things and the way we perceive.

And everything else is to facilitate that. Why? Nothing changes yet everything changes, and therefore Dharma is pervasive, meaning everywhere. Timeless, which means applicable during Buddha's time and now. Whether you are living in a village during Buddha's time with no water, no plumbing, no electricity, no Internet, no nothing, just a hut; or you are living in a great house in Bandar Utama[2] , with everything.

It's timeless, and at the same time it transcends all races, colour, creed, barriers, levels, classes. Why? Because all of us, in our own way, create or uncreate our realities, and what we perceive.

So therefore a person who is stuck on being happy, that they have everything, they're happy, they're comfortable, that is their own creation. Because it's their own creation and it's not real, when something happens, their world comes apart.

Similarly, a person on the opposite end of the spectrum, who doesn't want to do anything, who absolutely doesn't want to do anything with their lives, and they consistently fail and fail and fail and fail; they fail not because of circumstances on the outside or inside. They fail because of their perspective of themselves and the world around them.

▶ 2 Township in Kuala Lumpur, Malaysia

So, what happens is this: we listen to Dharma in order to get another perspective – of a person who knows better, of a person who has experienced better, a person who has traversed and passed the difficulties we have passed. We listen to a person who has more wisdom, who has more skill, and who has a broader spectrum, a thought, ideas and methods. We listen to a person who basically is free from wrong perspective, and that person can only be a Buddha. No other being except a Buddha can give us that method and that way to change our perspective.

Therefore, if we listen to the Buddha's teaching, read the Buddha's teachings, visually see Buddha, such as in images, it can help to transform our mind. But I want to stress – as I have always stressed, and all traditions of Buddhism stress – that Buddhistic practice or practice, is not incense, it is not altars, it is not statues, it is not prostrations, it is not water offerings, it is not doing Dharma work, it is not charity work. It is perspective.

Why? I will give you a clear example. There are people in Dharma, there are people in Christianity, there are people in Hinduism, whatever, who are very mean, who are not nice at all. But they know the rituals, they know how to chant, they attend the classes, they read the books. But when they deal with people, they are exactly the same as they were the first day they entered their religion.

And there are people in Dharma, in religion, in every religion, that when they enter the Dharma, from one week, the first time they hear their Minister, their Pastor, their Imam, their Guru, their Swami, talk about truth, you see their minds transform. Do you know how you see their minds transform? They are able to bear things that are not bearable. They are able to *tahan* things and put up with things they ordinarily will not be able to put up with.

Every single person that comes to you will leave you happy

I think every single person in this room is able to take things that ordinarily they wouldn't have been able to take. Think about you, think about yourselves. Okay, I hate to use this as an example, but think about the first time you met your teacher, and then now! How much were you cajoled, taught, compassionately advised, forced, yelled at, bribed, threatened, blackmailed into doing things now that you wouldn't have even imagined you would do. Just think about that!

And you know what's beautiful? There's a lot more coming! Isn't that fabulous!? Do you know why? Because you will reach a state where you can take everything, you can perceive everything, you can accept everything.

And what you give back is not negative energy, but positive energy, and that every single person that comes to you will leave you happy. You watch some people when you go near them: some people, we go near them we feel silly and stupid; some people, we go near them we're serious; some people, we go near them we are like "What's up?". Some people, we go near them we don't know what's going on. Some people, we go near them, we leave them and we feel very happy.

How we leave a person – confused, happy, sad, unhappy – is a state of that person's mind, and what their motivation is towards you. So if we usually leave a person feeling happy, that person's mind brings happiness to other people. If we leave a person confused, down, depressed, dour, angry, scared, that's the kind of feeling that is abiding in the person's mind.

So somebody comes near us, and after they leave us they are even more confused, we know that we abide in a state of confusion. We might go near someone and when we leave them, we feel like "What's up with them?" You know, we don't feel so good, we don't feel motivated anymore. Maybe we were very motivated until we talked to them, then we're like ughhh….. because why? They bring you down with their energy.

Some people we go near them, after we leave we feel very angry. We listen to their perspective, we listen to their brain, we listen to how they talk, their views and we feel, "Eww… why like that?" And some people, we go to them, and we leave and we feel happy. Not happy as in just jokes and jokes, happy as they give us something new to think about, a new way. And then we think, "Oh, I feel happy."

So just think, when we listen to the Dharma even once, when we listen to the Dharma two times, three times, ten times, twenty times, we will see our minds expand and grow. Definitely. If the Dharma is authentic, the lineage is authentic, the motivation of the teacher and the students – both, back and forth – are authentic, there will definitely be a transmission of the mind, definitely.

Some people can even come to a Dharma teaching angry, and leave released. Some people can come anxious, and leave released. Some people can come depressed and leave happier. Some people can even come with a mind that's not sure, and they can leave happy.

You see, we can't judge anybody's life, and we can't pinpoint anybody's life, and we can't say anybody is doing right or wrong. We can't, but the Buddha can. If the Buddha can't, why do we take refuge in the Buddha? So some people can very much say, "Oh you know, you can't judge me, you can't judge that person, you can't judge him, you can't judge her." Of course you can, if you reach a certain level of the mind.

So don't speak for the whole population with your level of the mind. *You* can't judge, and *you're* in darkness. But it doesn't mean everybody else is. There *are* beings out there... If the Dalai Lama comes along, or Lama Yeshe comes along, and says to you, "Oh you know, you are doing this wrong, wrong, wrong, and you should do like that and that person should do like that" and you say, "Well, you have no right to judge me," then who does? I mean, it's not right or wrong: you have to understand there are levels of attainments in people's lives and their minds.

So the Buddha *can* judge us, but not in the Western detrimental way. Judging is a negative word, but judging doesn't mean judging as in condemnation or condemning. It means a comparison of what we can do and what we are doing.

And that's what our Guru is for. Our Guru is there to let us know what we can and cannot do, and to cajole us, to inspire, to help us to do what we are supposed to do. Why? Why else would we seek a Guru? I'm sure we don't seek a Guru to fight with him. I'm sure we don't seek a Guru to debate on and on for the next twenty years about what's right and wrong, and get nothing out of it. I'm sure we didn't get a Guru to punch us. I'm sure we didn't get a Guru to get things out of him. I'm sure we didn't join our Guru to extort him, or blackmail, or cheat, or get something. I mean, that's not the reason we get the Guru. We can do that to everybody else in our lives; maybe we have!

But that's not what we do to our Guru. Why? He can offer us

something more exciting, much more exciting than blackmail and cajoling. What's that? A new perspective. A fresh perspective. So if you think about when you entered the Dharma, and you listened to the holy teachings of Lord Buddha, up until now, and if you've seen your mind expand, and you are able to bear things that you normally are not able to bear, that ability – from day one until now – is Dharma.

Not other people, whether *they* are practising Dharma or not; not your neighbours, not your friends, not anyone, but your ability to *tahan*. Now listen carefully: your ability to tahan people who are not practising Dharma, who are not doing spiritual practice, who are not good people; *your* ability to put up with them happily, continuously, is Dharma.

Whether we live for others, or we live on the basis of others, our attitude will be different

So that's the secret. Dharma is not you enter a group and everybody is fabulous, and they're wonderful, and everybody's enlightened. No, that's not Dharma. What is Dharma? Dharma is how much the other person does to you – within and without Dharma – and you don't become discouraged. Do you know why? Because your motivation was never based on them, your motivation is based *for* them. Not *on* them, *for* them.

If your motivation is based on them – "Oh if they practice, I practice" – then of course your mood will go up and down. If your motivation is *for* them, then whether they are up or down, you're up, and you want to make them upper, higher. Definitely. So we have to think very, very carefully.

When we're in Dharma, the proper motivation is essential from day one. Why is it essential? Because if you create the motivation for the sake of others – "I will listen to the Dharma. For the sake of others, I will study the Dharma. For the sake of others, I will read the Dharma. For the sake of others, I will meditate and pray and I will put up with difficulties. *For the sake of others.*" – then you know what happens? You don't become depressed, you don't become angry, and you don't give up.

Why? If we have someone we love very much like our children, our brother or sister, no matter what they do, do we give up? No. They can do anything – they can take all our money, they can ruin us, they can ruin our reputations, whatever – we never give up on them. I'll tell you why. Think about it! Because we are doing it *for* them.

We want them to be happy, we want them to have a good life, we want them to have realisations. So if it takes up to 30 years to give that realisation, even if we die and see them not realised, on our last breath we will advise them, "Take care" or "Do this or do that, don't let that person cheat you," or "Don't go with that nasty girl", or something. We will definitely say, even in our last breath.

You know, you've seen mothers dying: "Don't lose the crops... don't forget to water the crops!!" And they die! Why is that? Because they have never lived on the basis of you, they have lived *for* you. So whether we live for others, or we live on the basis of others, our attitude will be different.

So people who get upset easily, or they get into the little Dharma group and they say, "Oh, those people are all saints, I'm not going to do it!" You are not doing it for them! You don't say, "Oh, I quit the group because they are all so wonderful," because I have heard people like that: "Oh, they're too advanced for me, I'm getting out of here!"

And then I've heard people also say, "Nobody here practices, I'm getting out of here!" You see, that's the wrong motive, either way. I will tell you why: because you're not practising on the basis of them. If they are enlightened, there's another five billion people out there who's not! If they are not enlightened, well, join the rest of the other five billion people who are not! So our practice is not based on people or the group, it is based on *compassion* for them. For others.

So if we are going to think, "If they shout at me, I shout back at them;" if we have that kind of attitude, that's not a Dharma attitude. I will tell you why. It's not a Dharma attitude because it doesn't benefit them or benefit us. Very simple.

So when we want to do spiritual practice, it can't be on the basis of that, or on the basis of "*If* I have this, *if* I have that, *if* I get this, *if* that person is like that, *if* the group is like that..." Some people, when little things happen, they just drop out, they just disappear, they're just gone! Why? Their practice was not for anyone. It wasn't even for themselves! It was on the basis of people. Maybe socially they can get together, maybe it was an opportunity, maybe it was for fun, maybe it was for intellectual stimulation, maybe it was just for their own benefit, maybe it was just for "Hmmm, let's see what happens!"

But people who do Dharma practice not on the basis of, but for, their attitude will be different. The people who do spiritual practice on the basis *for* others, they will not be disheartened. They can go through *tremendous hardship and they will not be disheartened*.

They can go through severe beatings physically, and they will not give up the Dharma. Just as many people in Tibet were tortured, prodded by electricity, raped, emasculated, had their limbs cut off, beaten for them to give up the Dharma and they would not. They would not because they didn't practice Dharma on the basis of, "Oh, if my country is fabulous and there's nobody around that's harming me, I am going to be happy and practise Buddhism." No, because they practised for others, so they bore suffering.

For, example when we went to Nepal, we met the Great Tsawa Phutok Rinpoche, who stayed in jail for 20 years! He stayed in jail for 20 years and he is a high ranking Rinpoche but he was made to clean the latrines, the toilets of all the prisoners, because of who he was. And he told me he happily did it.

I asked why. He said, "Because I can absorb the sufferings of the three precious monasteries." I said, "What's that?" "Gaden, Sera and Drepung," he said. He said that every single day when he woke up in jail, he prayed, "May the obstacles of the monks and high Lamas and the Dharma to flourish in Gaden, Sera and Drepung come to me. And every time I get a beating, (which was a lot), every time I get scolded and yelled at by the guards, every time I am told to clean the latrine, I will bear it happily, because as I do it, I absorb their suffering, and I absorb their consequences and I absorb the obstacles of Dharma, and I am the one doing it."

And he said, "That's why I remained sane, happy, and I recited my mantras. There were times when I was caught doing my sadhanas and mantras, and I was beaten and punished." So he says, "I had to do it very skillfully, I had to lay down, pretend I was asleep, and learn how to do my mantras and prayers without moving my mouth."

I said, "Did that make you unhappy?" And he said, "No, it made it a little difficult, but I didn't become unhappy." And you can see he wasn't lying because you can see his face is very bright, very shiny, and very effervescent. And this is someone who teaches us Dharma by action, by example, not necessarily on the throne.

Repay the kindness of others by changing your attitude

So when you have a change of attitude, and you do Dharma on the basis of *for others*, you will not be disappointed, you will not be sad. You will not give up. You will never ever let go, and you can bear all difficulties, no matter what is said to you, what is done to you, what happens; even if you have to lose people, even if you have to give up people.

Lord Buddha lost his parents. Lord Buddha lost his wife and his child Rahula, his beautiful son. In ancient Indian tradition, your first son is a very big deal! Very, very big deal! And for him to lose his son, and lose his beautiful wife Yasohdhara – beautiful! She was the fairest in the land, and of course how many courtesans can he have?! And prestige, and power and money, youth, his beautiful body, his fabulous hair, his great clothes, the elephants, the armies, and all that he stands to inherit from his father…

Because these days, when we know our parents are rich, we're sitting there waiting for it. When, when, when? When are we going to get it? When, when, when? And we live our lives in such a way, "When, when, when? When do I get it? When?" The minute one of our parents pops off, you know, the traditional mourning (because we get paid for crying, because we are going to get an inheritance!) "49 days chop chop chop, Om Mani Padme Hum, see you later, hope you take a great rebirth, let's make a Buddha statue from KMT[3]. See you later Mommy, see you later Daddy. Can I have the money now?!"

And we pay off our bills, we pay up for who we want, we get our girlfriend, we get our boyfriend, we go out, we go to Australia, we go to America, we go to New York, we go to Honolulu, we go wherever we've been dying to go. "Thank God somebody died so I can *not* die waiting to go!"

And we don't actually think in that negative way, but subconsciously it's there. Why? We've been thinking like that for many lifetimes. We're

▶ 3 KMT – Kechara Mystical Treasures, one of the Dharma stores opened under Kechara House, the Dharma centre founded by Tsem Tulku Rinpoche in Kuala Lumpur, Malaysia.

dependent on other people. We don't take responsibility. We want things. So that's natural. It's not evil but it's natural. All of us, in one way or another; all of us have leeched off our parents in one way or another. All of us.

So, like that, every single person has been our parent, and every single person will be our parent again. And we need to repay the kindness of our parents in this life, past lives and future lives. Why? Who's more kind to us? The parents of previous lives, current life or next life? It's equal, isn't it? So how do we repay them back? By changing our attitude. How do we change our attitude? By doing things for others. And how does that repay their kindness? Because we collect great amounts of merit. And we don't collect negative karma and we can dedicate that merit to *all mother sentient beings*. And therefore we repay their kindness.

Yes! Every time we're aware, we repay their kindness. Every time we hold our anger and we reduce it, we repay their kindness. Everybody's kindness. Yes, yes, Melvin was my mother once. Yes, yes, Zahir was my mother once, a long, long time ago... I can't remember anymore. It was very traumatic. Yes, a long time ago. Milly was my mother once! Can you believe that?! I came out of Milly and she fed me and that time I am sure they don't have bottle feeding. And, just visualise this one! *Fat Monk was my mother once*!! Fat Monk! Monk Fat! FM was my mother, I suckled Fat Monk's breasts once, and he changed my diapers and cleaned my lower parts. Fat Monk was my mother once.

So I owe Fat Monk something. I owe everybody something. And therefore when we practise Dharma, we practise for others. When you have that attitude – *it's for others* – you will never give up. And do you know what? You will not give up on others as if you don't give up on your own children, on your own boyfriend, on your girlfriend, your wife, your parents. *You will not give up.*

I will tell you why: *a growing sense of universal responsibility opens up in your mind*. Universal responsibility. And that is, "I will bring happiness to everyone who comes to me. And whatever method I employ, whatever I have to give up, whatever I have to sacrifice, others are more important than me." Universal responsibility. And that's really wonderful. ...

Thrive on confusion, thrive on nasty people, thrive on weirdos!

So the purpose of our center has always been, is and always will be, to help people get knowledge to change their perspective. And whether they're Buddhist or not, it doesn't really matter, but to change their perspective because then suffering becomes less. So hence, for all of us to be motivated to read our little Dharma books, and watch our little Dharma DVDs, it's a little difficult because for every single lifetime we have been having a great time partying. And all of a sudden, someone comes along and says, "What are you going to do when the party stops?" It's a little difficult to stop, and just get off the turnstile or just get off the podium and start meditating.

But we need to do Dharma *for others*, please remember that. So, when you do Dharma for others, you don't say, "Oh, they did that to me, that's why I am not doing it anymore. They said that to me, that's why I am not doing it anymore. I went there and Wan gave me a black face and I am not doing this anymore. I went to KMT, and guess what, somebody was rude to me, I am not going there anymore. Oh, they're not organised, they're not ready, they don't have money, they don't have a system, they're mean, they're rude." We all complain about that.

Yeah! Welcome to Samsara! "And therefore I am not going to practise?" Silly! Silly, because you ain't going to find any place that has a perfect practice anywhere. *But* if we change our attitude, everything becomes perfect. I will tell you why: because everything that we encounter becomes practice.

And that's why, for Dharma practitioners like us, who really, really want to make a difference in our lives and the lives of others, we will thrive on confusion, thrive on anger, thrive on mischief, thrive on nasty people, thrive on weirdoes, thrive on people who are just totally out of it, and just test your patience to the end. We will thrive on it, do you know why? Because they don't disturb you.

Just think, before Dharma and after, how much you can *tahan* from people. Maybe before Dharma, if someone did something to you, you'd wallop them, you'd slap them silly, catch them in the parking lot somewhere and slap the crap out of them. But after Dharma, you *visualise* slapping them; you don't slap them anymore, just visualise. Then after a few more years in Dharma, you don't even visualise. You think, "Oh poor thing!" Oh Yes!

So with Dharma, you know what happens? You know what's Dharma?

Dharma is very beautiful, Dharma is to protect us. Protect us from what? Doing more actions and harm. So the more difficulties we have, the more we have an opportunity to absorb and transform.

And when we take refuge in the Holy Three Jewels, we are acknowledging to Lord Buddha, "I will absorb other people's suffering. Everyone's. I will take other people's suffering. I am happy to take it. And along the way I may fall down but I will stand up again, and I will fall down and I will stand again, but the point is I *stand up*!" That's what happens when we take refuge. So that's very, very important.

I am very, very happy to have these little classes because I enjoy very much sharing the Dharma with you. That's actually my passion, besides reading Dharma and videos and going to sleep early. My passion is Dharma and elucidating Dharma. I don't think of myself as a great Dharma teacher.

What I think of is this: for some reason I have some retentive ability of Dharma. I can remember Dharma quite clearly and well, and from many Gurus. And I would love to convey this to all of you because all of you haven't had the fortune yet to meet these Lamas, or probably never will because some of these have passed away.

So I may be able to do that, and I enjoy it. I don't know how to say it, I not only look forward to things like this. I enjoy it, I thrive on it, and I feel I have done something good with my life, after I have finished. When I go home from a Dharma talk, I actually sit there very high and very happy for many days. And I will talk about it with a few people around me, a few people who "force" me to have my foot massaged. You know, I'm *forced*. They're like, "*Please* can we make merit from massaging your foot?", and I am like "Oh, alright, here."

I'm on a high, do you know why? Because I did something good in my life. I listened to the Dharma, I absorbed some of it. And I retained, and I am able to share with others. And I feel really good, I feel very high. Nothing else makes me higher. And therefore, doing VCDs and tapes, and having a centre and Dame Khang[4] , all this – it's an extension of that. So I am happy to be recorded and taped and distributed, and encourage this in the writers' group

▶ [4] A smaller centre, attached to Tsem Tulku Rinpoche's home where he holds private audiences.

because I want the Dharma to go out.

I am not trying to be a star for the sake of being a star, because if I wanted to be a star, there's other ways to be a star. There's much, much better ways, much, much faster and easier ways, much, much better and I would have done it 20 years ago, when things were not prone to gravity!

So me wanting video tapes and VCDs and people and Dharma centre, and also our outlets, KMT, DMT, KP, YMT[5] , are an extension of this passion to bring Dharma to others, in any way, shape or form – writing, visuals, verbal, speech. It's a passion to bring Dharma to others. And then when I talk to other people, and when they do this, I feel passionate to talk to people who are passionate about that. Do you know why? Not because we share the same dream, because I admire that you also have compassion; that all of you have compassion, and I can draw inspiration from this compassion; that when we do Dharma work, we work very hard, and we don't give up, and we really pursue, because we have compassion for others.

So for even one person, I can become sick or whatever, talk to them, advise, it doesn't really matter, or give or help. Why? Because if that person can convey the Dharma to other people in some ways, then my passion is fulfilled. That's my passion.

And therefore hence all the stores, and the expansions. Even this furniture is an extension of this. Because if people see this, they will get attracted by this appearance, they come in, they want to know more, they learn more, they ask more, and then they want to learn Dharma more, and they transform. All this is for Dharma! Why else?!

The whole purpose of these gatherings, and the whole purpose of getting together, is to learn to do things for others, to change our perspective, to widen. That's the whole point, and that's why I am very excited to do things like that, and I am very excited to have people join all of us to do things like that. And I would like people who are effervescent, enthusiastic and really like to do, and really take their own share and take their responsibility, don't need to be pushed and prodded to do.

Do you know why? When you are not pushed and prodded to do things and you do things and you do it well, you know what it is? You are compassionate, and you want to repay kindness. When you have to be pushed

▶ 5 DMT – Dzambala Mystical Treasures; KP – Kechara Paradise, YMT - Yogini Mystical Treasures, three more Dharma stores opened by Kechara House.

49

and prodded, you have to be forced, it's a clear indication that you are not very compassionate, and you have to become compassionate. Because compassion begets compassion. It's very simple.

And if you make excuses for not learning the Dharma, or doing the Dharma, for any "valid" reasons – somebody was nasty to you, whatever – also it's not very good, because then you are doing Dharma *on the basis* of something, not for something. There's a very big difference when you do it *for*!

Imagine if I asked people to skip dinner…! They'll all get me!

It says in the *50 Verses of Guru Devotion* (all of us should read that, especially if you have taken refuge), "For my Guru, I can even give up my wife, my kids, my wealth, I can give up everything." You read that! That's not made up by crazy Tsem Rinpoche! I dare not! Imagine me asking somebody, "Oh, don't have a wife, don't have a girlfriend, do Dharma!" Oh, I'd get slapped silly! I got to look outside for booby-traps, they will get me! Yeah there will be a permanent Buddhist Jihad on me, I know everybody is going to get me.

Forget about telling them to give up their wife and stuff, I just say, "Can you give up one night a week to listen to the Dharma, maybe four hours?" Oh my God, to drag them here, to beg them, go there, drag them, cudgel them (like Kalarupa has a cudgel!), knock them out, bag them and drag them here and have them sit here, and give them jokes, give them fun, give them coffee, give them air-con, give them a nice room, give them a painted place, beautiful altars, give them all this - for them to come to listen to the Dharma. You have to *drag* them. They're heavier than a corpse. At least corpses, you just drag them; they hold on, they don't want to let go!

Oh yes, it's very hard, and that's what a Smuru or a real Guru has to go through to bring people to the Dharma. It is a monumental effort. And that's for one person – then you multiply that. Because each one of us, we have 108 reasons to kill our Guru, to get him. So imagine if our Guru says, "Do you think you can go vegetarian for one week?" and then he's got to duck! Oh my God, you'll throw a lamb-chop at him, "I am not going into vegetarian, I have been eating meat for my whole life!"

Then if your Guru says, "Do you think you can drive beyond 10 minutes to get to Dharma?" "But I live in Shah Egypt and it takes me five hours to drive there, and I'm not going there!" And then some people are like, "But I didn't eat din-din. I can't go to the Dharma talk, I didn't eat din-din!" Oh my God!

Or some people, "I think tonight I'm going to get laid." And then there are some people, "Oh, but I'm sleepy..." Or some of them, they profess they have bird flu. They go, "Ah-choo, I got bird-flu, I can't make it!" I'm like "What?!" Why? Because they look at a map of China, so they got bird flu, I'm like "Oh yeah, that makes a lot of sense!" And there are other people, "Well, there's someone in Dharma I don't like, and they disturb my mind, so I'm not going!" Oh God, so many excuses!

So imagine, a Guru asks you to come to a Dharma talk, you know how much effort it is on his part? Because he's asking for it, and that's just you! *One!* Imagine how many times you multiply that when you have a Dharma talk, how many people he has to deal with, how many SMSes and messages he has to deal with, the excuses – and that is just to help them.

And that's just small things – skip din-din, be a little late, be a little sleepy, maybe your lover scream at you, whatever – but heaven forbid if you ask them to give up their wife or their husband for the Dharma... Oh my God! They're going to be wearing "I love Osama Bin Laden *and Tsem Rinpoche*" t-shirts. And you know what that means! They are going to come look for me! The irony of these "I Love Osama Bin Laden" shirts – you know everybody hates him but they wear it just to taunt him.

Couldn't you see? Next year you're going to see me on trial, somewhere in America, I'm maybe like Saddam Hussein, I was pulled out of a cave, and I got overgrown beard and hair and I'm all disheveled. Then, "*He made me study the Dharma, he did!*" And all of you will be in the witness stand: "Yes! He made me study the Lamrim!" and then, flying Lamrims! And then the judge, of course, is Henry sitting there going, "Order in the Court, there will be no more throwing of Lamrim books at the defendant!"

Can you imagine that? Can you imagine the Guru *dare* telling them to live their lives differently? If I tell a student to live their life differently, do you know how much reaction I get back that's negative? If I tell them that they might be wrong, you know, they take the news and they wave it at me because I know what's going to happen to me when I go for the little boy's room … "Rinpoche found dead in toilet!"

Can you imagine that?! Imagine if I ask people to change their life, skip din-din, transform themselves, give up something. And you know what? I wouldn't dare ask for anything like that! No way! None of us are at that level. If we're at that level, we wouldn't have to give up our husbands or wives anyway. We would have no attachment. We can be without attachments and be happy!

See, during Buddha's time, the Gurus walked around and the students tip-toed around them. These days, the Gurus got to tip-toe around the students! Can you imagine that? Imagine his toe is like Baryshnikov, you know, always on ballet time! I went to see the podiatrist today, by the way! Oh yes, and then if you ask someone, "Can you please SMS me back the result? Pleeeeease…? I will give you Coffee Bean, money, and I will be nice to you, and you get to go home early, and…" Oh no, no, no, no, no. To ask someone to do something for you, it's a big No-No.

So if you tell them to change their lifestyle, if you tell them something wrong according to the Dharma, the yardstick of Dharma, *you will get it*. You will get it. Never mind asking them to sacrifice things that will bring them more harm, even when you can see clearly by logic, or sometimes by divination, sometimes by Dharma, you can see clearly they are going the wrong direction, and if you tell them something, they will think of 108 ways to justify what they are doing back to you.

And they will get you, they will justify to people around you, and they will keep talking and talking and bitching and complaining. Do you know why? Because they are not doing things for others, they are doing things on the basis of others. "If I get this, if I get that, if I get this, if I get that, then I will do this." Then therefore it doesn't constitute Dharma practice. Why? There's no transformation.

So, those types of people, they are not bad, but when something happens, they will suffer tremendously. Why will they suffer tremendously? Because they didn't do Dharma *for* others, they did it *on the basis* of others. *Big difference.*

None of us can check what we're doing and compare and judge other people's lives, but we definitely can set them in the right direction, because "judge" or "set them in the right direction" are just different words. Otherwise there will be no Buddha, there will be no Gurus, there will be no enlightened beings, and there will be no attainments. And that is to say that no one has attainments on this planet. No one! Then why have a Guru? Why? Why prostrate to a Guru who knows less than you? No, wrong. Wrong attitude.

So the purpose of the Dharma talks in this class is that we can get Dharma knowledge to change nothing, yet everything. And hence we have these classes. I enjoy it, I look forward to it. And look at the beautiful place, and look at how comfortable and nice it is! You know for us, our group, always something nice manifests, a nice centre, nice place. Everything manifests to receive the Dharma.

... EVERYTHING CHANGES

... Everthing Changes

We transform our minds because we love people

I want to offer you a small Dharma talk that will perhaps benefit you in your daily life and perhaps offer another perspective. I don't like to give Dharma talks that only benefit us for the Dharma centre or for doing Dharma work or just hanging around here. I like to give talks here that benefit you outside of here and I'll tell you why. Because most of your time is spent outside of here so what you do outside of here is more important than what you do here.

Here we dress up nice, we're happy, we're pleasant, we do offerings, we pray, we smile, we fold our hands, we recite mantras and we're very, very, very holy. Very holy. But when we leave here, that's when it counts. Some of us, when we're in front of the altars at home, in our office, wherever and we're chanting 15, 20 minutes, 30 minutes a day, we're very holy. Very holy.

We put beautiful offerings, silver, and we clean our Buddhas, we buy fruits (on discount because we're Malaysians, of course). We get our bargain fruits and we bring it back to Buddha and we offer it on the altar and then when we're at the altar, we pray. We fold our hands, we make sure we follow every line, we pronounce the word, if we miss a word we pronounce it again, we make sure we get that all right.

And we're very holy when we recite our mantras, and we honour it because we took the time to do it and to meditate and perhaps read, have a nice cup of tea and coffee, wine... I don't know, whatever you guys like to do when you're praying. (Me, protein drinks because I don't eat anymore!) In any case, that's very good.

What we do after our chanting and prayer is very, very important. So if we chant 15 minutes a day or half hour a day or one hour a day, that's very good, that's excellent. We should not stop because chanting reenergizes us. Chanting is something that is a phone call to the Buddha or a connection to the Buddha or something of an SMS to the Buddha. Yeah, SMS is better. Phone calls are expensive, SMSes are 10 sen[1] .

▶ [1] Malaysian currency; it is like the Malaysian equivalent of "cent".

So we send an SMS to the Buddha every day, it's very nice. It's like sending an SMS to our friends – we keep in contact. We send one once a year, they're going to think what do we want?... If we send it daily, then we're friends.

So when we do our sadhanas and prayers and meditations daily, it's an SMS to the Buddha daily. It's very nice, because why? We're not SMSing a friend that's unreliable, we're not SMSing a friend that we're not sure of, we're not SMSing someone that can change with their mood, with wealth, with fortune.

Some people when we have money, we're very good friends; sometimes when we don't have money, we see them later. Some people when we're good looking and we're fabulous and we're young, they're around us, and when we're not, they're not. Some people when we say nice things, they're our friends; sometimes when we don't say nice things, they're not.

So with Buddha, it is friendship, and his compassion and skill is unchanging. He doesn't depend on our mood, he doesn't depend on our status and who we are and what we are. He depends totally on his enlightened state of mind which is unchanging.

So what happens is this: we chant the prayers that were chanted by many holy Lamas, many holy beings and monks and masters and mahasiddhas and adepts and yogis and meditation masters, male and female, prayers that have been chanted for thousands and thousands of years. These prayers that we chant are not passed down to us from my grandfather to me, you know, like a home chicken soup for flu. No. This has been passed down from Lord Buddha to his holy disciple, to his holy disciple, all the way down to us. So the prayers that we chant are very, very holy and very, very auspicious and powerful because they originated from Buddha or one of his great disciples.

So when we do our chanting and prayers everyday, we connect or send an SMS to the Buddha. And what happens is this: we invite the blessing of the Buddha. And when we chant we don't feel the benefit immediately, for some of us. For some of us we feel the benefit immediately. But definitely long term, continuously, you will feel the benefit.

You feel a transformation in your body, you feel a transformation in your mind and you will feel you are able to let go of things more, you feel you are able to accept things more, and you feel your body actually physically healing, depending on what type of chanting or which aspect of Buddha, which energy we invoke upon. It definitely has blessings, definitely.

And we chant right or left, we chant good or bad, we chant English or Chinese or Malay or Indonesian, whatever, it doesn't really matter what language you chant in because the Buddha is better than the United Nations translators – he understands all thought, not just language. So don't think, "Oh, I chant like that, he won't understand." Some people think they chant wrong, he doesn't understand. Trust me, he understands!

Buddha's like a Vulcan[2]. He just touches you and he understands what's going on. He doesn't even need to touch you, he's better than a Vulcan. (But his ears are pointing down, not up!) In any case, we *should* chant, we should do our prayers and sadhanas everyday. If you follow that guideline every single day and you do it every day, it will definitely have benefits.

You exercise everyday, you get benefits. You diet everyday, you have benefits. You work everyday, you have benefits. So everything and anything that needs to be done in our lives, we need to do it every single day. We need to do it continuously and we need to do it with effort. When we do it continuously and with effort, then there are results.

When we do it sporadically, our results will be sporadic. If we go to the gym once every six months, we will look like we go to the gym once every six months. If we drive by a gym once every six months, we will look like we drive by a gym once every six months. If we go to the gym once every week, twice every week, we will look like that.

Similarly if we meditate and focus and practise and control our minds with the Dharma every single day, we will look like we control our minds. We will look like we are practising the Dharma. We will see transformation.

If we look at the Dharma once a week when there's a Dharma talk, when we look at the Dharma once a month when there's a Dharma talk, or when we look at the Dharma when we're in a good mood, when we get a bonus, when our friends are nice, we have a relationship, or when things are going well, or when things are going bad, and when we do it only at that time, we will look like we only do the Dharma when we're in a good mood.

So how much you do something will show. If you focus a lot on your

▶ 2 Character from Star Trek who is clairvoyant.

hair, your hair will look great. If you focus a lot on your body, your body will look great. If you focus a lot on food, buffets, the wonderful hawker food, you will look like you've been focusing on hawker food. If you focus on the Dharma, you will look like you're focusing on the Dharma. If you're focusing on retreats, you will look like you're focusing on retreats because your mind will be stable and firm and very direct.

You might be focusing on your mind and transformation of your mind to become better because you love people around you. You see, we transform our minds because we love people: we love our parents, we love our spouses, we love our lovers, we love our friends, we love people around us. So we transform our minds out of love. It's not something negative that we *have* to do.

So when we transform our minds, our speech is transformed. When our speech is transformed, we transform other people's minds and lives. So when we transform other people's lives and minds through our speech, that has to come along through our mind. So when that's transformed, it must be out of love. It must be. And what's more beautiful than to transform other people's lives through our speech? And that arises from our mind.

If our mind is always filled with untransformed qualities, then our speech will reflect that. And when our speech reflects that, the people around us and who we attract, how we can attract them, or how we can't attract them, will reflect our speech which reflects our mind. And that's very, very important.

So Buddhistic practice, spiritual practice is about transforming. Transforming our minds. That's very, very important. And if we transform our minds, whether you're here or outside, or whatever, you will make people around you happy and you will be happy. And that's very, very important.

So chanting every day is extremely beneficial and extremely helpful for us to do that. But the chanting itself is not Buddhist practice or spiritual practice.

The effect we have when we make another person happy without motive is Dharma. Let me repeat again: the effect we have on others when we make them happy without motive and when their mind is happy because of us, that is Dharma.

So some of us may be cleaning the centre, some of us may be doing books and writing, some of us may be involved in garage sales, and some of us may be listening to the Dharma, may be contributing money, or some people are contributing their efforts and time – that is so wonderful and that is so necessary and that is so incredibly helpful to everyone. But that itself is not Dharma practice. That is not.

Going to the temples and offering incense, and inviting monks to chant, and offering food and *dana* and robes to monks and nuns is beautiful and it's necessary and it's good and you should do it but that is not Dharma practice.

Dharma practice or Dharma is when our husband and wife and our friends and our associates are happy because we make them happy or if they're not happy and they see us for a few minutes, we make them happy. And when they feel this happiness and there's no motive on our side, that is Dharma. So if the people around us leave us confused, leave us unhappy, leave us in a quandary or we talk or act in a way that makes people more confused, that's not Dharma.

See, Dharma's nothing – it's not setting up altars or statues, it's not teaching other people, it's not printing a thousand books and giving it away every day. Dharma is when we make people around us less confused, more clear and happier and happier. And when they spend more and more time with us, they become happier and happier and happier. Do you know why? Because our mind abides in a state of joy. Our mind abides in a state of joy because we wish to bring joy to others.

And we can bring joy to others if we have controlled our mind. And we can control our mind if we take Buddha's teachings, Jesus Christ's teachings, Mohammad's teachings, Krishna's teachings. We take any holy being's teachings and we really, really, sincerely, not follow, but *practise*. Then you'll see a big difference. You'll see a huge difference.

If we simply go to temples, we follow high Lamas, we go for initiations, we run to this centre, we run to that Lama, we run to this puja, we do our little pujas and mantras daily and we talk about the Dharma, we read – that is very, very good but that is a very, very small contribution towards the practice of Dharma. It's necessary but it's small.

Why? You have to look at your state of mind and you have to look at yourselves and you have to look at your age and you have to look at the time you have left on this planet. Why? Nothing will stand still. Nothing. Young or old doesn't make a difference. Anytime. In some parts of the world young people die more than older people and faster and quicker. So there's no time.

We want more than a little pay cheque...

Let me give you an example of an athlete. An athlete will deprive himself of nightlife, relationships, fun, going out; an athlete will eat very certain foods, exercise six to eight hours a day, sleep early, not stay up. An athlete will restrict him or herself from friends. An athlete will deprive himself from many, many activities because they have to train and they have to work and they have to push and they have to discipline and they really, really have to transform and change their whole schedule in order to get their body ready so that four years down the line, or eight years down the line during the Olympics, they hope to be chosen, qualified – *hope to be*.

And then if they get in, they hope to compete honourably. And then all that discipline, all that hard work and dieting, all that incredible sacrifice of social life, all that sacrifice that they put in is for one medal. One little medal – a gold one, a silver one, a bronze one, hopefully a gold one. One little medal and a few minutes on the podium with your national flag going up and they play your anthem. And then after that, eight years is finished. It's finished.

And that is for something to achieve that is very small. And that's short lived. Because if they catch that athlete in a club… you know if it's a male athlete with three women and he's married – he's finished. "Oh, what a bad, bad example to all the children of the planet." Finished! So one teeny little mistake for all the work that he or she has done, *that is it*. They're finished.

So we want a little bit more. We want more than a little medal, a little more than a pay cheque, a little more than reputation. We want happiness and freedom from suffering. We want Enlightenment, nirvana. We want *Enlightenment*!

So someone who wants Enlightenment and someone who wants a gold medal… enlightenment means a daily affair, it means a life affair and it means every life you're Enlightened and you're able to benefit others tremendously. So in order to reach that state, don't you think that our efforts must be a little bit more than an athlete's? Let me be outright blunt: *much more* than an athlete's.

So some of us can work, put up so much energy into our business, so much time. We are a devotee of business and our Guru is money and the Buddha is our office and we go to our office and we hang out there 15 hours a day doing puja *all day*. When the telephone comes in, it's pleasure, when we write cheques, it's pleasure, when we look at our secretaries and people, it's pleasure.

We can do all this work and we can spend all this time in an office because you know what? It is our religion. We think it brings us happiness. But when we say, "Hey, you have to do a little bit of chanting"… Uh oh! The Lama or the Rinpoche who told that person that is going to have to run forth really fast because there'll be flying vases and rocks and chairs thrown at the Lama. "Go away!"

Lamas have a very dangerous job because Lamas have to tell people to get rid of anger – Oooh! Big one. The minute you tell them "Don't get angry," they throw a bitch fit at you. Oh yes! I get bitch fits – at least two or three or four a week – from different people, per week, every week. And I'm getting used to it. In fact, sometimes where there's not a bitch fit I look for one. I miss it.

And some of us… Oh incredible! I'm going to use the men's perspective. I'm not going to use the women's perspective because I don't know the women's perspective that well. But women and ladies, you're not out of this either, alright? Because you were men many times in your previous lives so don't think "I'm Miss Innocent here."

You see, some men are very, very interested in fabulous, beautiful women. They love beautiful women. They love fabulous, gorgeous women. They like them short and fat and delicious like a cupcake; they like them tall and thin and skinny like a sugarcane; they like them medium and well roasted and cooked. These men, they just love women. I mean, we all *love* women, we love our mother because if you don't love women, your father can't give birth to you!

So we all love women and men love women… (Uh, *most* men love women. In our group I have to say *most* men…! In our group, I have to say *some* women like women). My point is not what you like or who you like or the gender; I'm talking about the actual desire. Because what you like, who you like, who you are doesn't matter to the Buddha. The Buddha doesn't look at you in any such way.

So then for women, we will work very, very hard and have a lot of money so that we can impress them because we think very lowly of them, we think that if we have money, women like us. And there are one or two women out there who do think that way but that doesn't mean all women think that way. It means one or two *people,* who happen to be women think like that. But most women don't think like that, no. Anyway, we think that if we have a lot of money, nice car and we have a nice house, jewellery and we look good, that women will like us.

And women who like that, well it's going to be a lot of work for men to keep that up – *a lot of work*. All for just 10 or 15 minutes of fun and games, maybe two or three times a week. A lot of work. A lot!

And some of us, we like women so much and we celebrate so much that we keep a few women. Yeah, we have two or three, why not? "Because, you know, we love women and Buddha says it's okay, what! Buddha never said I can't have women," so we have two or three women.

So that means we have to work much harder and maintain much more in order to maintain more women because we're very generous. We love helping women! We're Bodhisattvas so we'll send money to women, or clothes or jewellery. We'll tell our other women we're not seeing women because we're kind, we don't want to hurt them, we're very kind people! We don't want to hurt this woman when *this* woman finds out that I'm with *that* woman. And then we got to tell *this* woman that these two women don't exist because we're with *that* woman. And we got to make sure when we're here, these two don't know about this one, and they don't know about each other because *we're kind*. Aren't we kind? Well, if they know, they're going to fight and create negative karma, what! We're Buddhists!

Just like the guy in the office, who spends 15 hours a day in the office – it's for the family, it's for all sentient beings, and it's for everyone so they're very kind to stay in the office 15, 20 hours a day.

And these men who like women, they're very kind because they figured that if they don't get all the women, they might be alone, they might not get other men, and then when they get them, they got to be very nice to them because they're Buddhist and they don't want them to fight. They want them to be happy – "May all sentient beings have happiness!" Yeah! I know a few people like that...

And then of course, they need to "donate" to these women. Because if they have three women, they have to visualise them as Tara, Vajrayogini and Singdongma. And they like to make offerings to them – jewellery, clothes, gifts. And they're very, very kind because they make a lot of offerings to these women.

And of course, that's a lot of work so that takes time away from mental development. It takes time away from spiritual practice and it takes time away from themselves. Because what happens when we "compassionately" take care of a lot of women is this: if our motive is to take care of these women and it's pure, that means that we are a walking Buddha. We're a walking Buddha, sitting Buddha, we're a sleeping Buddha, a lying Buddha.

If we're a walking Buddha and we maintain all these women, then what happens is that all of our energy and time goes into maintaining these women and getting things to maintain these women (because we're very generous, we're practising the six paramitas, aren't we?). We're very patient with them, we never get angry with the three of them, even if one of them catches us with another... we're very patient, we never get angry. And more, we can talk to them and explain why we have another two women. Very patient. Very kind!

And we have a lot of effort. You know why we have a lot of effort? Because we never give up. When one of them is unhappy, we talk to them, "Stay with me, the other two won't be involved anymore." And that takes a lot of skill! And that takes a lot of meditation because we actually have to think about it. We go to a very great temple like Starbucks or something like that, and when we're chanting our mantras – "mig mey tze wey..." we chant holy Lama Tsongkhapa – we think about how to talk to this one so that this one doesn't get angry, and how to meet this one so that this one doesn't know... It's a lot of work so when we chant, it can help us to help women. Very wonderful. And so a lot of our money will go to them. So money that could have gone to one person that would have done a lot of things for us, we're very kind, we disperse it to a lot. We're walking Mother Teresas! And not only that, then we need to get more money. So some of us, well, we need to get more money from different sources, different places so that we can take care of our women.

I've heard this for the last 12 years – trust me, I've had all types of very great Dharma practitioners parading in and out of my room saying, "But, you know, I got to do this to maintain my friend." I say, "Is your friend female?" "Um… I think so…" They're very kind! So you know, they need to work these hours, and then they need to do extra business deals, sometimes they need to do something slightly illegal. Slightly… But it's not bad karma because it's for women… sorry, for *maintaining* them. And they do more and more and they get used to it.

But if their motivation is 100% wonderful, they're walking Buddhas, well, why would they need women? (Well, okay, never mind, maybe I'm a little confused here?)

And then since they're not walking Buddhas and they maintain all this, it will be a lot of karma. There will be a lot of karma accrued because when these women don't understand our "compassion" and "kind and wonderful heart" and our extreme "generosity" in giving to them; if they don't understand and they misunderstand our Buddha intentions, they collect a lot of negative karma. Why? Because we hurt them.

"They're hurt, too bad because you know, that's their problem. They don't understand that we're a Buddha. But we're a Tantra Buddha that's why we have women, a lot of women." So we hurt them and when we hurt them and we deceive and we deceive people, then whatever practice we want to do, there's no effect. Why? If you're a Buddha, you don't need to practise. If you're not a Buddha, you need to practise. So it's either or, not both and not a mixture: "Well, I'm a Buddha on Monday, Tuesday, Wednesday; Thursday, Friday, Saturday I'm not." Doesn't work either!

We're all interested in sex, money and reputation

Same thing for people who are very attracted… I use that as an example because what are we interested in? All of us are interested in that dirty S.E.X word. Okay, let me say it: SEX! Okay, a Buddhist Lama here said the dirty word SSSSSEX! Right?

And what are we interested in? We're interested in money. What are we interested in? Sex and money, and some of us, reputation. So we want reputation, we want sex, we want money. That's not really bad because we're normal. We're not Buddhas. I'm not a Buddha, you're *not* a Buddha – we all want the same things. It's okay.

But you see, how we go about it makes a difference in the result. So whatever we do, however wonderful we talk and however we want to talk and say, it's very, very nice and a lot of people will believe us, but remember when we fold our hands to the Buddha, between us and the Buddha, it has to be clear and straight, otherwise there'll be no results. Why? We can only hustle around and bustle around at our jobs 15 hours a day. How many years have we been doing that? 10 years? 10 hours, 15 hours a day? How many years have we been doing that?

We've driven in the best cars, the best houses, we've had wonderful things, and then we go down, we go up… how many more years? What are we waiting for? What are we expecting? What do we want? What can we want that we already haven't had? What can we have that will bring what we want? There's no difference.

So people who are very into money – it's good, it's very good because people who are into money, people who are into women, people who are into reputation (that's about these three for all of us sentient beings in samsara – ignorance, hatred and desire. That's about it. There's nothing much); people who are very much into that and they say, "I don't have the energy to practise Dharma, I don't have the motivation, I don't have the patience, I don't have the effort," it's not true.

Every single person on this planet, every single person in this room has a lot of effort. You have effort to work very hard to make money, you'll work every single day. No one needs to motivate you. No one. You'll do it and you'll push yourself and you'll justify it with what? "Well, I got to maintain my family, my friends, my girlfriends, my boyfriend, my sister, my brother." You know you do have the effort, definitely.

And some of us, it's *a lot* of work maintaining our friendly female disciple friends. It's *a lot* of work, especially if we have two or three and especially if they're beautiful (because beauty is in the eye of the beholder). Some like them deliciously plump, some like them dry and skinny – it's up to you. I mean if you like them dry and skinny, it's beautiful, it's up to you. Samsara's samsara, who cares?! Some like them nice and short that wherever you go, you need to take a little chair so that you can talk to them, see and hear them. Some like them very tall so that you can carry a ladder around, up to you.

But the object is not the women, the object is our minds and how much we work toward them. How much effort do we put into grooming ourselves, making ourselves look good, getting money, giving stories to our other female friends and the energy at the time. How much time and energy do we put into these women? That's effort! And I'm not being sarcastic. You have effort. It's if the effort is directed at a place that will bring permanent, unchanging happiness.

You see, when Lamas sit on a throne, they tell you these things, they become your public enemy number one. If you don't like what they say, you will turn around and go and say other things about the Lama to get rid of them. Why? You don't like what he says. Or, number two, if you like the Lama, you'll say things to cover yourself. Or the third option is this: you actually surrender and practise. Those are the only three options.

So Lamas put themselves in a very precarious and dangerous position. They get people who want to kill them and get them for telling them something that they don't like, that can be harmful. Or they get ignored. The favourite thing is they usually ignore the Lama. They don't call, they don't SMS, they don't show up, they avoid. But behind they'll talk. Why? "Because every time I go there, the Lama's going to tell me I'm doing something 'right'".

So we usually avoid the Lamas, we avoid. But of course we have their pictures on our altar, we have their statues on our altar. We make prostrations, we wear their pendant, we recite their names, we have their name tattooed on our arm. You know, every time we go out, it's like "Tsem Rinpoche is number one!" When's the last time Tsem Rinpoche walks by and it's like "Isn't that your Guru?" You're like, "Is it?" You don't recognise him because you haven't seen him in a while.

Some of us get the Tsem Rinpoche tattooed as "Boss Lama", "Neon Lama", "Crazy Lama", "I hate Tsem Rinpoche" but the "I hate" is under the sleeve! So when Tsem Rinpoche shows up it says, "Tsem Rinpoche" and I'm like, "Oh! Thank you!" You get a tsatsa. And then when he's not around, you go "Hah..."

And then we have moods. You know, when we like him, when we don't like him. No point! Lamas are in a very precarious position because they, for whatever motive, tell us what the Buddha says and they tell us in a way that applies to us, that's kind of modern, with current examples and that kind of sometimes hurts. It's not meant to hurt. No.

No Lama will go out and hurt people. I'll tell you why. I'm a guest in your beautiful, fabulous country and I want to be a resident and I want to be here forever. I want to be a Malaysian. I'm happy here so why would I want to make a bunch of enemies and get everybody placarding? You know, with placards outside my house: "Get rid of that crazy Tibetan! Get rid of that crazy Tibetan!... because he told me I can't have three women, because he told me I'm a bad person."

Why would Tsem Rinpoche, or any Rinpoche or any Lama want to make enemies? No. But you see, it can't be that they're telling us things to make us hate them. It can't be that he's telling us things because he's got a motive. I mean, if he's got a motive, wouldn't he tell us things we *like* to hear? Maybe he passes an *angpow*[3] to help us maintain our compassionate deeds towards women.

But maybe if a Lama is very, very nice and wants to get on our good side and gives us money or jobs or whatever, so we can get some money to maintain ourselves and our friends and our women and our females and all that, and he's very, very kind, it's in order for us to realise, to transform, to practise the Dharma.

So whatever we want to say, whatever we want to do, it doesn't matter. You can keep pictures of your Lama, you can praise your Lama, you can make pendants, you can make advertisements and websites. You can do whatever you want.

▶ 3 Angpows are little red envelopes traditionally used by the Chinese in which money is put and presented either as a gift or a sign of respect.

Ultimately the real way is facing ourselves and making a determination that "All the things that I'm doing that create unhappiness in others, I'm going to stop. And all the things that I'm doing that create happiness in other people, I will increase." I'm talking about Buddha happiness, not samsara happiness: "Well, if I have five women, they're very happy because I'm with them, or I give them money and that's happiness! I'm a Bodhisattva! I'm Buddha."

Well if any of you believe that, come see me. Let me give you some robes, Buddha robes so you wear it when you go see your women. We'll give you a yellow Lama Tsongkhapa hat so you can go there because you're very, very compassionate.

And some of you who like to go to the office because you're very compassionate, please wear Buddha robes and Dharma hats and go to the office because you're very *compassionate*, you know, you need to show who you are. Why not? You can't be in disguise like me all the time, wear funny clothes and run up and down the street, Bukit Bintang[4] , waiting for phone numbers and pick-ups and all kinds of weird people… you can't be!

No. I told you, I'm one of these Rinpoches that bought my certificate. Not from His Holiness, not from anyone holy like that. I bought my certificate. Where? I don't know… Um, I know, someone was walking by and they dropped their certificate, and someone else found it and I bought it from that person.

Do we want happiness?

So what we need to do is this: we need to make a decision. Do we want happiness? And do we want to make people around us happy? And I'm talking about real happiness. If we do, in today's case, as in every other religion, it's possible. We need to follow Buddha's principles.

If we're Christian, if we're Muslim, if we're Hindu, it doesn't really matter – all is beautiful. But we need to not just talk about the principles and love the principles and respect the principles and have the principles and understand it and teach it, or listen to it. We need to uphold it and practise it. Why? Then the real cause of becoming happy will be better.

▶ 4 A section of the city centre in Kuala Lumpur.

So all of us have effort. All of us. All of us can do it. We all have effort. Some of us, in getting boyfriends or girlfriends, we are very persistent; some of us in keeping a relationship, we're very persistent; some of us in working very hard, we're very persistent. And none of that is good or bad – please don't think I'm being sarcastic, I am not. If I want to be, you know I'll be straight out about it. Anybody who knows me, they know I don't beat around the bush. In my garden there are no bushes and trees, I just go straight to the end. Some people go around the bush, go round the block, up the tree and then back and then you go, "Oh my God, why don't you just tell me?!" I don't have any blocks, any trees, and no shrubs. I go straight to you. I'm in the Sahara Desert so what you see is what you get.

So my point is this: that we need to take stock of ourselves before it's too late, before we lose people we love, before we lose the respect of people that love us, before we lose our Lamas, before it's too late to practise the Dharma, before unhappiness sets in.

We need to start. Why? It's never too late. Never. Why do I say never too late? Because you don't look at your lives in conjunction to this life. You have to look at it in the spectrum of universality, of many lifetimes. This is just one step in your continuity of many, many lifetimes. So it's never, never too late. That's one.

Second thing is we're all here and we want to practise and we want to help and we want to contribute, and a lot of people in this room have contributed and helped in Dharma in many ways: by effort, by praying, by coming, by cleaning, by washing and by donating and effort – a lot!

For example, Uncle Lai. Uncle Lai here is an elderly retired man, respected, with a family, his kids are grown up and he's okay. But he comes weekly as part of the cleaning committee to clean. This respected older gentleman does not have to come and clean the place, but obviously he has something spiritual inside that he wishes to clean a holy place to collect merits, so that everybody can gather together to have a beautiful and wonderful environment to practise this Dharma.

And that's all Uncle Lai can contribute at this time. I'm sure he would like to contribute a lot more, for whatever personal reasons – it's none of my business – but I respect the fact that he even comes and contributes just cleaning. An elderly Malaysian man, educated and retired, comes and cleans. And normally if we're retired, we're supposed to be respected and taken care of, our kids come and kowtow and take care of us and watch us. But he can come weekly and clean. I didn't tell him to do it. I think he volunteered on his own. No one needs to hound him and ask him. I'm not praising him. I'm just using an example.

However we wish to help, we can help if we want to help. If we don't want to help, we'll have many ways to say we don't have time. Well, Tsem Rinpoche can say he doesn't have time because I'm more busy hanging out in Dome in Bukit Bintang and flashing my LV bag. (That's very important. Very, very important! Why is it important? Because then people will "respect" me!)

So then when we do Dharma work – you know why we do Dharma work? It will benefit many people, we will spread the word that brings happiness to many when we do Dharma work. And when we do Dharma work *together* – not hiding somewhere alone and saying that it's Dharma – but together, it inspires other people. It inspires people because when there are more numbers, it inspires!

So if we say we have nothing to offer and we should be at home, or we'll do something else, or wait until we have something, and then, "I'll show up when I have something," how do you know that you *won't* have something? How do you know that? How do you know when you do have something, they need it? Or how do you know that you will ever have it?

So just showing up for pujas and activities and help, it encourages people tremendously. It inspires people tremendously. And in that way, and that way alone, you benefit the Dharma. Just showing up and listening and contributing. Please don't do Dharma *your* way. Please do Dharma according to Buddha. Please don't make up a whole set up of scriptures and teachings – a new *Lamrim. My Lamrim.*

Please follow the original *Lamrim*. Please. Why? Even someone like me who sits on a big throne and wears robes and has a big name and title, all that stuff, dare not make up a new *Lamrim*, a new book. I dare not. Because, well, in the Taoist tradition, there are these little white and black fellows with long tongues, and when you die, they come and visit you! Well, I don't want those guys with big tongues coming and licking me and taking me to nowhere! So

I'm a little scared of those two fellows with the long tongues!

So when we do Dharma work, we do it and we contribute any way we can. We don't wait for a certain time, we don't wait until we can or cannot. Listen to your Lama. Your Lama tells you to get involved, don't make up any other excuses – valid or invalid – not to. Your Lama requests, begs you, asks you and folds hands for you to do it. So do it!

And the Dharma tells you to do it. And the Sangha needs you. Who's the Sangha? The people who are involved. They need you. So don't make up your own set of teachings and rituals. Follow the ones that were already set off 2,500 years ago by the Buddha. That's why we need a Sangha, that's why we need spiritual friends to support each other.

If you can't even bear the people around you, how can you bear everybody else outside?

May I also let everybody know that when we do Dharma work, the key here is this: we do not do Dharma work based on other people or situations or environment. We do Dharma work *for* other people, *for* other situations and *for* other environments.

Let me reiterate: if we do Dharma because the group is wonderful and they're kind and they're gentle and they're soft, and that's why we want to do it, we're not doing Dharma. If we're doing Dharma because we're informed and people are organised and people are doing everything perfectly, and then we do it – that's not Dharma. That's more dependency, where actually we're in a little club.

You see, we should do it whether the person or the group is nice or not nice. I'm not talking about them being extortionists, you know. They bring in women from China, and then they sell marijuana and then they pilfer in drugs from Cambodia or Burma or wherever they pilfer it from, I'm not sure. And then, we say, "Oh but it's Dharma and I can't give up..." No, no, no. I'm talking about normal situations – for example, in our Dharma centre.

It's new and it's filled with a lot of wonderful, professional, educated, fabulous people. Fabulous! If we put our hands together, we can do a lot of things. But if we sit there and wait for this person, or that person, or that person, and this person, we can't. Why? Everybody cannot make everybody happy. But if we put our efforts and energy together, we definitely can make a very powerful – in the sense of beneficial – centre, for many, many beings.

And we have to do that Dharma work: we don't do it when the centre is nice or organised, and there are no cancellations and problems and difficulties, and that if there are any difficulties and problems, we run. Do you know why? Then we're not doing Dharma for the correct motive. We're doing it because we're basing it on something. We have to do Dharma *for* others, not *based* on others.

See, if there are people in there who are doing things that we don't feel right about, it should in fact motivate us to practise the Dharma, to work harder, to do more so that we can inspire them by example, by result and eventually attainments.

So if we say, "That person in the centre's like that, that person's like that, that person's like that and therefore I'm not going to get involved and I'm not going to do it, I'm staying away," wrong! Then the whole basis of your Dharma practice is wrong.

Why? Dharma practice – as His Holiness the Dalai Lama has said many times – is for others, is that we can bring benefit to others. That's why the rule of our centre is *The Eight Verses of Transforming the Mind*.

Those *Eight Verses of Transforming the Mind* is the pith of *Lamrim* and the pith of Buddha's teachings and the core of what we believe in. We are all not practising that, that is for sure, including me. But because we have that goal and ideal, we have hope to go on.

You see, you don't give up your job because you're not rich. You keep working until you're rich – whatever rich in your definition is. So if you say, "I'm not rich, I give up," how stupid!

So how can you say, "Oh, people in the centre, or certain people in the centre don't practise the *Eight Verses of Transforming the Mind* and therefore, I'm not going to do it." That's all the more reason you should do it, that's all the more reason you should be involved, that's all the more reason you should practise. Do you know why? Because you're not practising on the basis of you getting this, this, this and this. You're practising on the *basis* of "Because this doesn't have, you wish to give."

So if you can't practise patience with your own Dharma brothers and sisters and you can't practise perseverance and effort and forgiveness with your own brothers and sisters – your *own* ones – how can you benefit all sentient beings? How can you say that, "I'm a Buddhist and I'm going to go out and benefit the world?"

So why do you go see your Guru? Why do you fly to Tibet to see your Guru, wherever you fly to or helicopter to or walk to or take a boat to or swim to? What's the point of going to see a high Guru? Why tell people, "My Guru is His Holiness, the living incarnation of Buddha himself, the *living Buddha*, Tsem Rinpoche!" Why? If you don't practise Dharma? Because they're going to look at you, they're going to look at Tsem Rinpoche, they're going to say, "Can you both take a boat back to Tibet?!" What's the point?

So if your Guru is the highest one in Thailand, the highest one in Cambodia, highest one in Tibet, Nepal, India – these great Gurus in these countries – and you yourself are not high, you yourself are doing everything opposite, then you bring your Guru down. Why? If your Guru is so high, why can't he affect you? Why can't he transform you? Why? So that's how students destroy the Dharma.

So therefore, if you don't go to a centre or you don't get involved and your excuse is, "Because this person is not good, that person is not good, that person's evil, this person lied to me, this person tricked me," and then you don't do it and you don't go: *wrong motivation*. Please let me tell you why. Because without these people, how do you develop the qualities to benefit others? How? If you can't even benefit or *tahan* or take the people around you, that are close to you, how can you take everybody else outside? How? You can't.

Then you must think in this way – that at least these evil, bitchy, difficult, sarcastic, greedy, very complicated people are in the Dharma centre making an attempt towards something better. That's better than everybody else who doesn't make an attempt. Much better.

So if we say that, "They're not organised, I'm not going," help them get organised. In fact, you should be motivated, it shouldn't demotivate you because then your motivation was wrong from the beginning. *Wrong.* So, "They're not organised, they can't do this, they keep having cancellations."

Well, you know what? Guess what? They're human beings too.

Let me tell you a little secret

Guess what? I got to let you guys know a little secret: *Tsem Rinpoche is not a Buddha*! I know! I know you guys are like, "Oh my God... really?!" Tsem Rinpoche is not a Buddha. Tsem Rinpoche is not even a Bodhisattva... Oh God! Here we go! "We've been lied to!" Tsem Rinpoche is not even an arhat! Tsem Rinpoche is not even a pure Dharma receptacle. Oh my God!" Okay you guys know now, it's out! I'm like Princess Diana telling you about my bulimic problems.

Here we go. Look! I've had these problems and all these public engagements.... and you know, I've had to go for these blessings and I had to pretend I was a Buddha, and I didn't want to because I need those angpows to pay for my LV bag! But I'm going for rehab, I'm going for counselling. I'm seeing Doctor Tsongkhapa and I'm talking to him.

Yes! I need to tell you guys the truth: I am not a Buddha. I am not a Bodhisattva, I am not even an arhat, I'm not even a good little Dharma student. I am just like you but I took 18 years out of my life to study the Dharma while you guys were on the beach looking at beautiful women and men. I was looking at beautiful people too but I interspersed it with Dharma. So that's why I'm on the throne telling you things and I get the angpows and you don't!

So my point is this: I am not a Buddha and I've got anger and hatred and jealousy and desire and problems and complications and headaches – I have all of that! I'm sorry... You know, somebody evilly made a statue of me here for you guys to pray to because it's to mock me, I know. Why would we pray to someone who's not a Buddha?

But no, all jokes aside, I'm *not* and if I'm not, I don't think anybody in this room is a Buddha either. And you know what? We got to stop expecting ourselves to be perfect and the people around us to be perfect because we're all not Buddhas. Maybe you all need a hanky to wipe and come to realisation, wipe your snots away!

And we will have cancellations, we will have problems, we will have setbacks, we will have difficulties, we *will* have miscommunications. We will have problems and we will have teething problems and it will continue as the place grows and grows and grows – it will continue.

Why? If a mother and father have one child, they have this many problems; if they have two, they have this many; if they have 10, they have this many problems. So similarly, if the Dharma centre has five people, it's going to be very organised. If you have 50 people, it's going to change; if you have 500, it's going to change. So as the centre expands – and that's what's happening – the teething problems expand.

So we can avoid and abandon and go away to say, "Oh well, because they did that to me, they said this to me, I was dishonoured, I wasn't appreciated, nobody looked at me, nobody cared about me."

Please don't think like that because you know what? I could think the same thing – everything you feel, I feel, and it's exaggerated by many hundreds, for many years – I don't feel like that because I don't feel I'm in the Dharma as a career or as something to make money from or to get something from the Dharma. I'm in the Dharma because... well, I'm not a Buddha but I do care about people and I do like people and I really don't want people to have problems and if I can help them, I will do it. And I mean that.

I really do care about people a lot so I'm in the Dharma because I care and the only way I can extend my silly care, my limited care is by giving Dharma because if I give Dharma, I give everybody the method on how to find new food everyday. I teach you how to plant crops and when your crops are great, you're set. And then I can hit more people and teach them how to do more crops.

So I'm not a Buddha and I'm not a Bodhisattva, I'm not enlightened but I do care and I do wish to help. I'm not in the Dharma to make money, I'm not in the Dharma to get name or reputation. I *need* money, I *need* reputation, I *need* to look good, I *need* this, I *need* that to promote Dharma because *initially* no one's going see who we are.

They're going see the outside, and outside, if you look good and you're alright, it equates Dharma is good. This is for some people initially. Not for people who are more advanced in Dharma. For people more advanced in Dharma, I can show up smelling like garbage, with ticks and lice, they'll still prostrate. But I don't think I can do that in Malaysia. You know, they'll probably call the health authority on me!

But in any case, the situation is like that. So when we're in the Dharma, go in, please don't base your help, your contribution, your participation and your practice and what you do on *who* is in the centre because sometimes we will get people who are very capable, with no time; and sometimes we will get people who are not capable but they're doing their best. But the fact that they're here, it's alright, so that if we do something based on one person, or two people, or we talk and we gossip, we don't increase our own negative habituation.

Everything changes, and yet nothing changes

So what we need to do is we need to forgive, consistently and constantly. And we need to contribute and participate; not based on others but we need to contribute and we need to be involved and we need to do because we find that Lord Buddha's teachings make sense: "It's modern, it's logical, it's beneficial and I receive some benefit and I would like to share this benefit with other people, consistently."

And when we do this, we are doing Dharma *for* others, not based on others. When we do it based on others, we will always get depressed, unhappy, stop, begin, go away, don't want, think negative things and we're always pointing fingers at others. When we do it *for* others, irregardless of what happens, we will not give up and we will not stop.

And you know what, don't think that that's something monumental. You're already doing that. Irregardless of how your kids are – for most of you – you will not give up. Your kid can be a little rotten monster, killing birds and insects and putting nails in the schoolteacher's chair and not doing homework and failing every subject, and talking back to you, you will still feed your little monster and love it and hug it. Only a mother can love it. You will. Why? Because it's yours.

Similarly, what am I trying to say is: you have that determination. You know, that's for beautiful mothers. For men, once they commit themselves to a woman that they love, no matter what – sick, cancer, well or not, fat or thin – they will stick with that person and they will be with that person and support all the way. And I've seen many examples of that too.

So similarly, we *do* have that quality. We do. All of us have the qualities I'm talking about. I'm not waiting for you to develop it. I'm just asking you to redirect part of it – not all! – redirect part of that effort and that enthusiasm you have for women, money, job and reputation. Just take a teensy little bit out. I'm not asking for much – about 45 %. You're like, "45%?! That's almost half!" Alright, alright, 44%!

Redirect it towards others. I feel that I have some Dharma to share with others so if we combine and you redirect that energy with me, I'm like the magnifying glass that can burn something in the sun that is focused on it. Burning in the sun directly is difficult. I'm like the magnifying glass so I can concentrate the energy and I can burn something for you under it.

So what happens is this: if we combine our energies and we work for others, it changes our whole perspective. And my favourite saying is, when we have the attitude of not being based on others but it's *for* others, everything changes and at the same time, nothing changes.

Nothing at all changes, but everything changes. Why? Our whole perspective is different. That's what I would like to share with you all. Not a scolding, not an indirect reprimand, not to put anyone down. No. I don't need to go around the block to put people down. I'm famous for that! I'm famous for being mean and bitchy and rude and direct and difficult and temperamental and cancelling things on the last minute...

Yes, I'm a Tibetan diva! And the diva-ship is going to grow bigger and bigger. I am a Tibetan diva. And if you don't like it, too bad! Don't you love it? See? You found out: I'm not a Buddha. I confessed it! I let it all out so you guys know because some of you are thinking, "Hmmmm I wonder which Buddha he is." I know none of you thought, "He's not," you just thought, "*Which Buddha? Is he Mahakala? Is he Yamantaka?*" Nobody ever thinks I'm Shakyamuni or Tara or Tsongkhapa. Nobody ever thinks I'm one of these... Oh! These guys will never get upset, they always sit there, smile at you no matter what. Get on my nerves!

I like these ones which are kind of dark, one of these Buddhas that are the Diva Buddhas. Yes, the Diva Buddhas: they're dark, they're red, they're fierce and they have flags, they want clothes, they want their own room, they want red lighting. Oh my God! They're *Divas*! So we have Diva Buddhas and then we have Buddhas. Setrap is a Diva Buddha. You don't give him his own room, he gets pissed off. He's already pissed off, he's always pissed off... a good pissed off though. He needs a red room.

So people used to think, or think, that I'm an emanation of a Diva Buddha. Well, I've come out and told the truth, very Diana, Princess of Wales. Bless her soul, she's not with us anymore... I'm not going to write a *Candle in the Wind*, I'm going to write a *Butterlamp in the Wind* song for her, you know? That's right, that's very Tibetan. So this butterlamp is gone. Mine is not going to be a butterlamp. It's going to be propane gas! You blow, you can't blow me out!

Listen to your wisdom voice. Don't listen to your habitual voice

So we need to work for the Dharma, work for our teachers, work for the centre, work for others not on the basis of how others act, talk, speak and treat us but in response to their harm, we work even more. So when you see someone in the lower state, you work more, you do more and you plot and plan more how to help them. Why? That's what Lord Buddha taught us. That's what His Holiness the Dalai Lama teaches us. That's what we're taught.

And in our centre, like a hospital, we're going to have weirdoes, freaks, strange people, people with bad motives, people who have good motive with a bad motive behind, peacocks, giraffes, elephants, swine, we're going to have rich and poor, we're going to have beautiful and not beautiful, we're going to have all types.

And you're going to have people who are dressed well, some are smelly, some are fat. We're going to have all types of people, but you know what? That's what this is all about. You don't allow people into the hospital on the basis of race, gender, sex, if they need healing. You allow them into the hospital of Dharma because you don't want people to suffer.

So whether they're rich or poor, good or bad, evil or not, fat or skinny, tall or short, it doesn't matter. Whether they have a good temperament, whether it takes them ten years to transform or one year to transform, whether they transform or not-it doesn't matter. Why? In fact, them not transforming, them not changing, them not becoming better, fuels you to do more meditation, more practice and more ways to help them.

And if we can help even one person in our Dharma community, we gain so much: we gain the ability and the knowledge and the effort to help so many others. To complain about others in the centre, to write letters and to say this and this, and to have fear and trepidation to do Dharma work is totally the wrong attitude. Why? In fact, those should feed you to do more.

If you live in an environment of no fear, no trepidation, everything is beautiful and fabulous, why do we need to do Dharma? Why? Why practise what you have achieved? If you're Bill Gates, do you think you need to open up Kechara Mystical Treasures on Piccolo Mondo to make some money to supply your Dharma work? Do you think you need to?

So why would Bill Gates come and say, "Well I need a nice happy working environment and I can't pay too much and it's got to be like this…" and he gives you all kinds of conditions when he's the richest person on the planet (he thinks…)! Why?

So if we make conditions to our Gurus, conditions to the people, to ourselves and to others, we self-demean our practice because it's a clear indication that we have gotten the wrong direction of our practice. We're not bad but we need to redirect ourselves. Redirect.

So what happens is this: the people who complain, the people who have difficulties, the people who are bitchy and problematic, and the people who don't transform, and the people who create gossip and problems – forgive them and love them and by your example, transform them and by your persistence and effort of not giving up, give them hope and courage. Not criticise and gossip and talk about them, and write about them, and say things about them, but in response to their harm, give them benefit.

If we do that, then this life will be happy and future lives will be happy. And that's the purpose of our centre: to invite all the weirdoes, invite all the fruitcakes and invite all the people who can't find themselves, or the people who find themselves and we wish they *didn't* find themselves.

Invite all the people who didn't find the right "themselves" and all the lazy and all the evil and all the ignorant people – all these people, they're people, and they deserve Dharma, they want happiness just like us. And we're not much better than them either, we can't judge.

We need to invite all these people into our centre. And they will be an object for us to practise to become real Buddhists. It is only when you fall down you can see how strong you are. When you fall down and you stay down, and you complain, you bitch and you make people feel sorry, you want people to give you this, give you that, it shows you your lack of strength. It is when you fall down and you're humble and you push yourselves and you can never stop, that's where it shows that you really practise.

Therefore, we don't need an altar, we don't need a picture; our Guru is in our heart. And that Guru is not Tsem Rinpoche. That Guru is our good qualities we already have and we need to make them bigger. Listen to your wisdom voice. Don't listen to your habitual voice. Listen to your wisdom voice. Don't complain about bad things.

You know why? In our centre, we have a lot of bad things. Do you know why? Because we're a bunch of amateurs! Hello! *We're a bunch of amateurs*! We didn't have a centre for the last 600 years like Gaden monastery which is run perfectly and fabulously. We're amateurs! Rinpoche's an amateur. I told you, I'm not a Buddha! I'm going to wear a t-shirt from now on: I'm not a Buddha! Maybe think about a catchy tune, I want to do a rap song: "He's not a Buddha! *clap clap* He's not a Buddha! *clap clap*"

So in any case, my point is this: why complain about this person and that person? Please don't. Please put your hands together and work for each other and others and grow and share and expand. And don't stay away using excuses that "*That* person is wrong. *They* make me feel guilty. *They* didn't appreciate me. *They* didn't do this for me. *They* didn't give this. *They* hurt me." No, don't. If you really, really felt like that, you wouldn't be here today. If you really felt like that.

So stop using that as an excuse to go back into wrong habituation. Help others. Help and contribute. I, as your Lama, if some of you have accepted me as your Lama, please don't put pictures of me on your altars or whatever. Please show up and contribute in Manjushri class and Migtsema[5] when you

---

▶ [5] Manjushri Classes are weekly Dharma discussion sessions held at the centre; Migtsema sessions are twice-weekly sessions of chanting migtsema mantras.

have time. Because your showing up will make your Lama happy, if he happens to be accidentally enlightened along the way, maybe this week or next week, (maybe he's not, never mind)…

And don't criticise your Lama, don't criticise your Dharma brothers and sisters and never carry tales back and forth. The minute you say something negative – even if it's true – you allow yourselves to fall into that trap. Never. And be honest with your spouse, your girlfriend, your boyfriend, your husband, your wife, your lover, whoever. Be honest with your spouse. Be honest. And don't hurt them because karma does return.

And help the Dharma; don't help the Dharma based on things going well. Help the Dharma based on things *not* going well. When things don't go well, help.

Why? When your kids are having problems, why would you go away? Why? Why would you abandon them when they're having problems? No. And don't have conditions to do Dharma, or don't have conditions on when or how. Don't. You know why? Because there's so many people, everybody's so special, they have their special type of needs and approach and problems, and we need to overcome each way in order to master and to help another being. We need to do that.

So please don't make it a condition that it must be like this, this and this. "Perfect, organised and no cancellations, and money and everything is easy and no fundraising and therefore, I'll do it." No, please.

In the midst of chaos, we are still happy

You got to where you got to because of challenges in your life that pushed you to where you got to. You got there and you're here. Similarly, all these things are beautiful challenges because the difference between doing Dharma work and normal work is in the end, you make people happy. In normal work, you just get a pay cheque which is pretty good too but that happiness doesn't last. So if we can do both, that would be wonderful.

Don't do it on the basis of someone. And that goes for your job, that goes for your family, that goes for your personal relationship: don't do it on the basis of this, this and this. Do it *for* others. *For!*

This Dharma talk applies to your daily life, applies to you, applies to us and this is not me talking down to you because I'm so "wonderful." This is what I learnt from my wonderful Gurus, that since I'm in this position to share, I will share with all of you.

And then if you really practise and put into effort what I have just spoken about, you will see your complaints become less and you will see that the people around you who listen to your complaints become closer to you and they notice the change. And you notice that you forgive people more and you find yourself more accepting; and then accepting of your own situation and other people's situations.

And you know what's most beautiful is that a lot of our projections of how we expect things to be will start to go away and we start seeing reality, the way things really are. And when we see things the way they really are – not what we *wish* them, or want them or project them or force them to be – we'll experience happiness and joy, that in the midst of chaos, we are still happy, we have strength and we'll be able to help others. And this strength comes from inside, not based on the outside.

Someone like His Holiness the Dalai Lama, who absorbs so much suffering from people, listening to their problems daily for the last 50 years, losing his country, being called a fox in monk's clothing, being dethroned, being said negative things of, no respect as the king of a country, nothing. Losing his whole empire, his whole country, his whole people and seeing his people suffer and tortured and mutilated and killed, and them coming to him saying, "Hey, help us! Help us!" And he absorbs this *daily*.

Yet, just as the Venerable Tenzin Palmo had said, when we go see His Holiness, when we look into his eyes, we see love and we see happiness. We don't see sadness. He's not happy about what's happening but he gives happiness because happiness is not based on what happens on the outside, it's based on inner practice.

And we can have that quality, and if we practise the Dharma it will be possible. And how do we start? Every single day, we recite Lama Tsongkhapa's Guru Yoga, by hook or by crook. I mean, you brush your teeth everyday, no matter how busy you are, right? You take a poop everyday, no matter how busy you are, right? You got diarrhea, you go to spend more time taking a poop, right? And everyday you take time to take a pee. Everyday you definitely take time – some of you take a *lot* of time – meditating on buffets, lattes. And some of us, two or three times a week we have "special tantric" sessions – we all have time! We all have time for this.

Well, we need to find time (and we don't need to find, we *have* time) to do our sadhanas every single day. A sadhana is for self-transformation. Do Lama Tsongkhapa's Guru Yoga every day. Not "lalalalalalalalala." Concentrate, meditate. I gave a CD talk on it, two times, it's recorded. Get it. Listen to it, listen to the commentary on how to meditate. And practise that, recite migtsema (Lama Tsongkhapa's holy mantra) daily if you don't have your personal sadhana. And do that every day, by hook or by crook – you're pissed off, you're happy, you're sad, whatever you are. *Every day*.

And for people who are old and people who are dying, to recite the mantra and blow on them very gently. On animals that have died, to blow on them gently. And to absorb. Why? By doing that, you will have an SMS to the Buddha which you will get blessings back that will help you to have courage to move on until you reach a stage where you don't need a Buddha's blessings. You will reach that stage. Definitely.

So please don't do things on the basis of this person, that person, this, that; or don't do it on the basis of this, this, this. Do it for others, not based on others. So that's our new mantra here: *Om Do Dharma Work For Others Not Based On Others*. Then when we think like that, a lot of our little things just flitter away. A lot.

And if you don't have time, then please don't poop today, do your sadhana! And some of us don't eat today (and some of us can *not* eat for a few days, let me tell you!) and do your sadhana. Just do your sadhana, you'll find the time. Think along those lines.

GET OVER IT!
MAKE MISTAKES... THEN FACE THEM

Get Over It!
Make mistakes... then face them

────────────── ° ──────────────

This Dharma talk follows a public apology made by one of Rinpoche's close students, Geraldine. Geraldine had left the Dharma centre and not been involved in the centre's activities for about two years due to certain misunderstandings and unhappiness with the centre on her part. Before a public Dharma talk, Geraldine made a formal apology to Rinpoche and his other students and made a request to return to doing Dharma work.

We can't change the world but we can definitely transform our view of the world

Dharma work is a very, very difficult job. It's just as strenuous and just as time consuming, if not more, than every other job. So therefore, it is a very, very difficult job because in Dharma work (if you're doing real Dharma work) you're not just teaching people how to do mantras, you're not just teaching people how to pray, you're not just teaching people how to meditate, or tell them to read a good book.

When you're doing Dharma work, what you are doing is you're trying to solve people's problems. Not solve their problems just symptomatically – if someone has a spirit possession, and you do some rituals and you do some prayers and you teach them some meditations, and if they do it, they will be freed of the spirit possession. It's not as simple as that. You have to go down to the cause – the cause of people's problems, the cause of people's difficulties. It's not outside enemies alone, it is not someone cheating you, it is not someone lying to you. Outside enemies alone is just environmental. It is something that manifests. In life, from the time we're born until we die, we're going to meet and we're going to encounter people, we're going to encounter situations that we seemingly think make our life very difficult.

But when we look at it: yes, there are difficult people out there; yes there are complicated people out there and they will do their best sometimes to make our lives difficult, but *how* we react towards that is how much suffering we create for ourselves. When we react negatively back to others, and we react the way we normally act, without Dharma; when we react negatively without Dharma, we create more harm for others and we create harm for ourselves.

And it doesn't end because we get them, they get us, we get them, they get us. And then you may think, "Well, why should I stop? It's not fair, it's 50-50, they should stop also." But when we know Dharma, or when we have come under the grace of Jesus Christ, if we have come under the grace of Buddha or Allah, when we have adopted a form of spiritual practice; even if we have not – if we have "adopted" our parents (if we don't believe in religion and we're atheists, that's fine also) and we have "adopted" our family name, then not to disgrace our family name.

And if we have a wonderful country like Malaysia, where everybody's educated and everybody's civil and everybody's very, very, very, very good people, not to disgrace our country, not to disgrace ourselves and disgrace our families, our wives by acting in a manner that reciprocates their harm with harm. When people harm us, we should stop them but we should not reciprocate vengeance or harm on them.

So what happens is when people do negative things to us, because we are older, if we have some grey hair on our head, if we are matured, if we have gone through the hard knocks of life, if we have especially learnt the holy Dharma, we have a very special duty not to react back to other people the way they react back to us. Why? It takes one person to stand up and say no. Like the Buddha says, if someone gives us a gift, we don't need to take it; we don't need to take that gift.

So my point is this: we can't change the world and we can't make the world do or act as we think they should do or act. But we can definitely transform our view and projection of the world. If we change our view and projection of the world, it's as if the world has changed. Whoever is trying to harm you, you do not harm them back and you say, "I'm sorry" a lot and you smile and you're humble – their harm will stop.

It's not a matter of you being right or wrong. It's a matter of stopping harm. So what happens is all of us – including me – *all* of us, we have good points and we have bad points in us, and sometimes the bad points take over because of certain situations, certain people or certain ways we think, or mostly habituation from the way we've grown up.

So the way we've grown up and the way we've encountered things affects us and the way we react to other people. So like that, we make mistakes and sometimes when we make mistakes, it's a very, very big thing not to admit our mistakes; it's a very, very big thing not to say, "I'm wrong" or not to let the other person win. By not admitting and not letting the other person know that we were wrong, we may think we have won, we may think that we are right but actually we create a lot of suffering for ourselves because we have to make a lot of explanations to cover, to cover, to cover, to cover.

And eventually, no matter how much we explain, no matter how much we talk, we will be "found out." And we become, inevitably, unhappy. So Lord Buddha teaches us not that there are no enemies out there; Lord Buddha doesn't teach us that there're no enemies and everything's our fault. No. That's illogical. What Lord Buddha teaches us is that there *are* enemies, there *are* people, there *are* difficulties, there *are* difficult situations, from the time you're born until you're dead, from the people who are the poorest and humblest to the people who are the wealthiest – their problems are going to be exactly the same, the way it manifests to them.

Yes, we all make mistakes. The key is to face them

So my point is this: we all slip, we all make mistakes, we all do things that we regret later. The key to that is not to *hide* our mistakes, the key to that is not to be oblivious to or try to go away from our mistakes. It is to face it and to make amends with the people that we have hurt and the people we have damaged.

And sometimes we say, "But I didn't mean it that way." It's okay, most of us don't mean to hurt but if the hurt has been done, from their perspective they've been hurt. So if from their perspective, they've been hurt, we have to question ourselves: what did we do? How did we act? And what words did we say that hurt them?

Because you have to understand maybe some people, when they were younger they were shouted at a lot by an elder and they have lots of low self esteem. So when we give them a slight angry look or we tell them like, "Oh! Go away!" they might be *very, very* hurt because they've been used to that their whole lives, been put down in that way so that when we say something as simple as "Go away", it might hurt them.

Whereas a person who has self esteem and confidence, when we say to them "Go away" they say, "Okay, I'll see you later, I'll see you in a little while."

People react differently. From our side we didn't mean any harm, we don't mean anything bad. No, we don't. But sometimes people may take it wrong. So the issue here is not who is right or wrong. The issue here is we are *one*. The others are many.

So instead of trying to make the others fit into our scheme and our thoughts and our projections and the way we think things should be, *we should try to fit into others'*; especially if we're practising Dharma, especially if we want to practise Dharma.

The real practice of Dharma is not the wealth of a Dharma centre, the physical growth of a Dharma centre, that the Dharma centre becomes bigger, bigger, bigger, that the temple becomes more wonderful and fabulous and there're huge crowds and it's just thousands of people seeing your Lama – that's not the growth of a Dharma centre. *Anybody* can do that – businessmen can do that, false priests can do that, anybody can do that. Anybody can draw a crowd as long as you have something to say because there are many, many types of people out there.

It doesn't matter if the crowd is big, it doesn't matter if the centre is large or huge, it doesn't matter if the centre is wealthy or not. Of course if the centre has sponsors and help and assistance and it can grow, it is sincere, it will be of benefit to many people. But the *real* growth of a Dharma centre is individual students and teachers seeing their mistakes, facing up to their mistakes and expressing and apologising and healing. That is a growth of a Dharma centre. That's what we want from Kechara House[1].

▶ [1] Kechara House is the Dharma centre established in Kuala Lumpur, Malaysia, by Tsem Tulku Rinpoche and for which he is the spiritual director.

Kechara House or Dharma centres or churches or temples – all that should cater not to people just coming in and putting a joss stick, and then praying, "Give me luck, give me fortune, let me find a girlfriend or a boyfriend." No, it's not that. A temple or a church or a holy house is holy because it teaches you to be different than what you've been taught. And so in a Dharma house when someone – teacher and student – finds their mistake and examines it, and if it takes them one day, one week, one month, one year, one decade to find their mistake and they face up to it and they own up to it and they talk about it: that is the growth of Dharma.

Why is that the growth of Dharma? Because Dharma grows when our mind transforms to something better, something much, much better. When our mind improves and faces itself, when we take responsibility – when we take responsibility for what we're supposed to do, when we take responsibility for our emotions and our speech and we take responsibilities for our mistakes, that is Dharma growth.

What is Dharma? Dharma is right attitude, right conduct, right thinking. So when someone makes a mistake and they can face it to themselves, that is the most important. Telling other people is wonderful but facing it to themselves is the best because when we face our mistakes, then we are on the road to Enlightenment. Why is that? That mistake will be removed, it will be filled with wisdom.

You're not bad. There's another point of view

So that's what I want in a Dharma centre – growth. Inner growth, spiritual growth. I want husbands and wives to be very close; I want husbands and wives who have been estranged, for difficulties or arguments, that have gone apart, to become close. I want husbands and wives to become very, very close.

And I teach that type of Dharma because most of you will not be priests and monks but if we can be a happy, harmonious husband and wife, the children are affected. And if the children love the parents, the father and mother, then the children will grow up with dignity, self-esteem, right view, right understanding and example.

If we ourselves are a bad example and our children only see that, how do you expect them to act? If our children act negatively, it's a reflection of us, most of the time. Why is that? If our children are estranged, if our children are naughty, are not taking responsibility, are doing things that embarrass us and we're angry, to be angry at our children and to keep them at a distance will not help them. I'll tell you why: because now they're young we can control them. When they reach 18, 19, 20, their minds come forth, they meet with other friends, they meet with other peers and they say, "Look, your parents are like that, what for? Let's get outta here," then you will have no control over them.

While your children are young, you should give them advice and talk to them. Not just worldly advice that they can hear from TV or from movies, but advice that is higher – the Dharma. And how to give that advice is if *you* know the Dharma; and if you know the Dharma, not only repeating what the Buddha has said but actually *practising* the Dharma from your heart. Therefore you will become an excellent example for your kids.

And you may think they're your kids, you had them, they're your responsibility. You produced them, nobody forced you, no one threw them at your doorstep, so if they grow up alienated or cold or away from you or they feel difficult, it is your responsibility to make them close.

So my Dharma teaches people in a very gentle and respectful way, that you are not bad but that there's another point of view. So it teaches children to be close to their parents, it teaches parents to be close with each other, it teaches people to be close with their relatives, it teaches respect of elders, it teaches respect of the law, it teaches respect of who we are as a human being and other human beings.

In my type of Dharma, we do retreats, we do meditations, we do chanting, we do all of that because those things help us to focus our mind on what is correct. But the real practice of Dharma is – at your level – harmony within the family, harmony with each other, harmony with your kids, harmony with elders, harmony with the law, harmony with your neighbours and everybody around you.

And therefore, in my house – Kechara House – whether you're a Hindu, you're a Christian, you're a Buddhist, if you're atheist, it doesn't matter. You don't have to convert, you do not have to say I'm your Guru, you do not have to say you're a Buddhist because all that is completely irrelevant. What is relevant is not labels that are stuck onto you – "I am a Buddhist. I've converted. Tsem Rinpoche's my Guru."

All that is irrelevant. What is relevant is when you become closer to your wife and husband, when your difficulties are resolved, when your children start to listen more and more because they watch your own example, through time and consistency. Not once or twice but *consistently*, that you can sacrifice your pleasures and what you like to do, your free time for the sake of your children.

And when elders are respected by people who are younger – that should be the way. Whether elders are right or wrong – sometimes they're humans too – if they lived this long, they survived this long, they deserve our respect. And it's beautiful in Asian culture that we respect elders very much and I am very for that. There needs to be some order in society.

And also my brand of Dharma is to respect the people around us and the people that we meet. "Whenever I associate with others may I think myself the lowest among all and hold others supreme from the depths of my heart." That's very important. This is called *The Eight Verses of Thought Transformation*. That is the heart of the Dharma, that is our credo, that is the motto of our centre.

What happens when the moment of anger is over?

So therefore, people who can face up to their mistakes and confess – they're not confessing to the Guru, they're not confessing to us. They're confessing to themselves. And when they can confess to themselves and they can face up to it, there's growth. You see, sometimes when we admit our mistakes, people may react negatively or positively to us and we may say, "Well, I confessed and they're still nasty to me." That's not the point.

The confession is not how *they* react to *you*. It's you facing up to what you have done out of your anger and hatred and jealousy and desire (because we *all* have that. We *all* have jealousy, anger and hatred at some time in our lives). But when we get angry, when we get jealous, or we get revenge and we fight, at that moment it's very good but what about when we calm down? Do we want to be accepted back? Do we want people to love us? Or do we want us to be estranged?

Because you see, anger is impermanent. We don't want anger. Disharmony is impermanent but once that's over, where will we be? And that's more important than the moment of anger. So when I get angry I always think, "Do I want to go this far? Do I want to carry it that far? Do I want to do this?" Because why? I know the next day or the next hour or the next minute, my anger is going to go down and when it goes down, how do I feel? How will people accept me? Will they feel the same about me or will they lose respect for me? And that's very scary.

So when we want to go have fun and we abandon our family, after the fun we still have to come back to our family. Do we wear away at their respect? Do we wear away at our husband's respect, our wife's respect? Do we wear it away that when we come back after our fun, our anger, whatever we're doing, do they still respect us? And if we work so hard and we have so much and the family doesn't respect us, what's the point?

Then the kids grow up empty. I know that, I come from a broken home, I've been adopted twice over, I ran away from home when I was 15 due to heavy abuse. I came from a very, very difficult background. I'm not talking about coming from a golden childhood so I know what it is to have parents or not to have parents. I know what it is.

So my point is - this is not criticism. You come here on a Sunday afternoon and evening, you could be watching TV, you could be sitting at home relaxing, you could be driving around, playing golf or whatever you're doing but you've taken two, three hours out to listen to wisdom – this one helps you, this one helps your family, this one helps your wife, this one helps your husband, this one helps yourself.

Why? I will speak about wisdom, and how we grew up in life is people giving us knowledge. From the time we were born, from our kind, beautiful parents to our teachers in school, and to our elders and our aunties and uncles who give us wisdom – all this has formed us to what we are now. And even people that have harmed us have given us tremendous kindness because they teach us how our mind reacts.

Geraldine

So we have a wonderful Dharma centre now – air con, beautiful floor, beautiful images of the Buddha. This didn't manifest because of me. This manifested because of everybody's hard work – the committees, the liaisons, the volunteers, the staff, all the people who worked past, present and future.

But before all of this manifested, there were a few people who stuck by my side, 24 hours a day and worked very, very hard. They are on my beck and call 24 hours a day and if anybody knows me intimately, I'm a very demanding, difficult person. Once you join me, you can say goodbye to personal freedom! I have a middle name – it's called Tyrant. Yes. I am a drill sergeant. I am a tyrant. I am a monster. And I have no sense of time, order or freedom for anyone. Once you join me, that's it. *That's* it. A few people tried to protest and make noise. Futile! Futile, doesn't work.

So my point is this: Geraldine and Chia (and there are a few others, but I'm just mentioning these two) have been with me for many, many years and worked side by side with me. They're my valet, they're my butler, they're my driver, they're my court jester. Yes, they get my food, they're my cook (don't have Geraldine cook for you… but never mind!), they're my shopper, if I get pissed off, they're the object I throw things at. I mean, they take *all* the abuse.

And not just mine, they have to take abuse of a lot of people who come. And then when one person asks them a question, you think that your question is solved, you're happy. But you see, they have to answer the same question for hundreds and hundreds of people, year after year after year. And they always have to have a smiling face, they always have to be perfect, they cannot have their bad days, they cannot have that time of the month, they cannot have difficulties, they cannot frown – they have to be perfect.

So people like Geraldine and Chia have to be perfect. And they can't slip and they can't have any emotions and they can't have any anger and they can't show anything wrong because they have to be perfect. Why? When they face all of you, if a hundred of you have experienced their kindness but one person has experienced their bad hair day, then everybody's going to make noise: "Oh, why like that? Why like that? Why Dharma like that? Why people like that? Why their assistants like that?"

But you have to understand: my assistants are people too. They have limits too. They work very hard also. And they don't deal with one person, they have to deal with many people. And Geraldine and Chia, for many, many years didn't have a salary, didn't have a sponsor and we lived very, very frugally. You should see the car we drove in for *years* – it's not even a car! And there were many times the car just doesn't run and doesn't move.

I'm not kidding. One time they were taking me to Mid Valley Shopping Mall. Just a couple of hundred metres before Mid Valley, it just stopped. That's it. It just stopped. Why? Nothing. Not like your sophisticated car where it goes "Beeeeep! No engine oil. Beeeep! No battery." It just stops. So Geraldine, Chia and I had to combine our psychic powers to figure out what's going on! Yeah! *For years.*

For years we lived in little crappy small apartments and ate bread (don't look at Geraldine, she had bread *and butter* too. She somehow snuck some butter into her diet). And for years we just wandered around on buses going to Singapore, here and there, teaching the Dharma and spreading the Dharma but we had a dream, which was to bring the holy Dharma to the educated wonderful people of Malaysia.

So Geraldine physically was not here for two years but mentally she was, I believe that. And therefore, Geraldine was angry before and Geraldine was not happy about some things before. And then she decided to manifest that anger by going away and by protesting and saying this and that but I don't see that as bad, I see that as normal. All of us do that. All of us have done that. All of us need that.

I don't think any one here has the "right" to forgive her, not even me. I don't think this is about forgiveness. I think this is about a person who says, "Look, I did things this way and it's not the right way and I'm going to do something else," and I think this type of person is not confessing or is not on trial or is not here to prostrate to a big Guru from Tibet and have him say, "Oh, you're forgiven."

This person is practising Dharma right now and I think this person shows us a good example. Yes. This person shows me and all of us a good example and it is wonderful that someone can say, "I made a mistake."

All of us are superstars

And let me add one more thing to that: most of us in this room – except a few of us – are Malaysian. And for Malaysian people – with respect – face is a very big thing. Not to be wrong in public although you're wrong and, everybody knows you're wrong; not to be wrong with your friends, with your family although everybody knows you're wrong and silly but to give you face that you're not wrong. Why? If you lose face, you lose everything. I don't know why. I really don't know why. But in a Malaysian society, losing face is a very big thing.

And for someone in a Malaysian society to come out and say, "I'm wrong," in front of hundreds of people and people you don't even know and people you *do* know, is Dharma. Why is it Dharma? It's not about forgiveness or wrong or right. It's about moving on, it's about benefiting others and it's about when one of us feels down, it's okay. It's okay to feel down, it's okay to be wrong, it's okay to make mistakes, it's alright to be angry. It's *alright*. Do you know why? Because we are not Buddhas.

So what we need to do is we need to support and help and care and love everyone. Geraldine is requesting her work to continue again with Dharma but her Dharma work has never stopped. Why has it never stopped? Because if it wasn't for people like Geraldine, we would not have what we have now. Definitely not. And I'm not complimenting her, I'm not complimenting anyone. Do you think Tsem Rinpoche can do this all by himself? Definitely not. I can just teach the Dharma. That's about it.

So my point is this: Dharma practice is when someone improves their mind, when someone grows and someone expands. And you know what happens? They don't lose, they're not "forgiven." They win and they accept themselves and they grow. And when they grow, the Dharma grows. It takes one person, another person, another person…

We don't all have to be so dramatic and come up with flowers and all these things and blah blah blah blah blah, and then make a big speech and song and dance, and tears and tissues and Kleenex – we all don't need to do that. But what we need to do is when we all make a mistake – and we all do and we all will again and again – face up to it and make a change. And that's all that matters.

Of course Geraldine's welcome; she's never been unwelcome. No one's unwelcome. In the house of Buddha, how can anyone be unwelcome?

So I commend Geraldine for practising Dharma. I commend Geraldine for facing up to herself. I commend Geraldine for all her help in the Dharma in the past, without which all this would not be possible. No one can sit on a throne, gloriously proclaiming the Dharma and never reflecting on the kindness of others and what they have done. All of us are superstars and all of us have a job and all of us can combine to spread the Dharma and we need each other to do it.

Glossary
——o——

Amitabha – The Buddha of Infinite Light.

Arhat – A being who has realised Emptiness.

Avalokiteshvara – Also known as Chenrezig (Tibetan) or Kuan Yin (Chinese). Buddha of Compassion.

Bodhisattvas – Enlightened Beings/Buddhas who out of their great compassion "come back" to samsara to help sentient beings out of suffering.

Buddha – A fully enlightened Being. To attain Buddhahood is to attain a certain state of mind that is free of samsara and all suffering. It is not just Buddhists who can attain this; every sentient ·being has this potential to become a Buddha.

Chenrezig – see Avalokiteshvara.

Dakinis – Literal meaning is "Sky Walkers" or "Sky Goers." Dakinis are the personification of subtle enlightened energies and often likened to angels in the Christian faith.

Dana – An offering made to the Sangha or the Guru.

Delusions – Our projected realities of the world and phenomena around us that are not necessarily the Truth.

Dharma – Literally, "Right Conduct." Dharma refers to a certain truth based on teachings established by Lord Buddha 2,500 years ago which help us to understand and cut away suffering, and to bring about happiness and total freedom from suffering. Dharma does not refer to just Buddhist teachings but also to teachings in all religions which give this same message of a "right way" of attaining happiness and bringing benefit to others.

Dharmapala – see Protector

Deity - In the Buddhist context, this refers to the manifestations of the enlightened mind. Manjushri and Tara may be considered "deities," not in the sense of gods but as enlightened Beings.

Drepung (Monastery) – See Gaden

Eight Verses of Transforming the Mind – see *Appendix*

Emptiness – To realise Emptiness is to see that there is no inherently existing self, no subject or "I"; everything is interdependent.

Enlightenment - A state of mind which is free of all delusions and which has fully activated the inherent potential of limitless compassion and clarity. To be enlightened is to be free of all suffering.

Gaden (Monastery) – Gaden, Sera and Drepung monasteries are the three largest and most prominent monastic universities of the Gelug tradition and are over 600 years old. Gaden was founded by Lama Tsongkhapa and was relocated together with Sera and Drepung to South India and continues to flourish today.

Gelug – A school of Tibetan Buddhism which was established by Master Lama Tsongkhapa in the 14th century. It is affectionately known as the "yellow-hat sect" and follows the teachings of Lama Tsongkhapa, namely Lamrim Chenmo or The Stages of the Path to Enlightenment.

Guru – Spiritual teacher.

Guru Yoga – Yoga literally means unification so Guru Yoga is the practice of aligning and unifying our mind with that of the Guru and Yidam.

Heruka – Fierce tantric form of Avalokiteshvara.

Ignorance – This is not a derogatory term and does not refer to what is usually termed "stupidity." Ignorance, being the opposite of wisdom, is what the Buddhist considers one of the three main negative afflictions of our mind which causes suffering. Ignorance harms us, for without wisdom we are unable to effectively deal with or come out of our self-created sufferings.

Karma – The universal law of cause and effect (its direct translation from Sanskrit is "action"). This suggests that all positive, negative and neutral actions of our body, speech and mind will have a corresponding reaction. As long as we are in samsara, we are subject to the law of karma. Only upon being enlightened can we be free of karma.

Lama – Spiritual teacher.

Lamrim Chenmo – The Stages of the Path to Enlightenment, a text written by Lama Tsongkhapa that outlines the precise steps we need to take to attain Enlightenment.

Mahakala – Wrathful emanation of either Manjushri or Avalokiteshvara.

Mahasiddha – Highly attained Dharma practitioner and master.

Mandala - A symbolic representation of the universe. To make a mandala offering to the Buddhas is a symbolic offering or visualisation of all that is precious within the universe.

Manjushri – Buddha of Wisdom.

Mantras – Words that are the spiritual energy of Buddhas in the form of sound and which evoke the energy of the Buddhas.

Merits – The result of a positive action done without personal motive. The beneficial energy gained in this way will not be exhausted but propels us further on our spiritual path.

Migtsema – A mantra that invokes upon Lama Tsongkhapa, and the three Bodhisattvas he embodies: Avalokiteshvara (Buddha of Compassion), Manjushri (Buddha of Wisdom) and Vajrapani (Buddha of Power). See Appendix for the full mantra.

Mudra – Hand gesture expressing an aspect of enlightened activity.

Nirvana – Sanskrit for cessation. The complete cessation of suffering and freedom from samsara.

Offerings - We make offerings of the best materials we can afford to The Three Jewels as a way to collect the merit to support our spiritual practice. By making offerings to a higher enlightened being, we are effectively making the prayer to attain the very same qualities they embody. Examples of offerings could be precious items like silver or jewels, flowers, light (candles), water, food etc.

(Six) Paramitas – Also known as the six perfections. Enlightened qualities that help us to progress in our spiritual practice and eventually attain Liberation from suffering: Generosity, Patience, Ethics, Joyous Effort, Meditative Concentration and Wisdom.

Practice – Practising the Dharma functions on two levels: 1. The outward practice of making offerings, prayers, prostrations etc. to the Buddhas as a way of connecting to the Enlightened mind. 2. The inner practice of transforming the mind to develop the positive enlightened qualities of the Buddhas, such as compassion and wisdom.

Preliminary practices – Practices that are done to prepare for higher tantric practices and that help to affect the transformation of the mind. They are water bowl offerings, prostrations, Vajrasattva purification mantra, mandala offerings and Guru Yoga, each to be done at least 100,000 times.

Protector (or Dharma protector) – Protectors are enlightened Beings in fierce forms that sometimes emanate in a form that is "closer" to us and that concentrate mainly on helping us to accomplish Dharma works and to clear obstacles to our Dharma practice. There are also protectors who are unenlightened, but bound by oath by enlightened Masters.

Puja – A ritual of offerings, prayers and mantras. Pujas perform different functions such as purification, removal of obstacles to Dharma work or to establish a stronger connection to the Buddhas.

Refuge – Submitting oneself fully with total faith and trust in one's Guru and in the power of the Three Jewels to teach and help us traverse the complete path to Enlightenment.

Retreat – To retreat from worldly activities of body, speech and mind to focus on spiritual development.

Sadhana – A collection of prayers and mantras which are to be recited on a regular, daily basis and which seeks to transform the mind by cutting away negative states of mind and developing enlightened qualities.

Samsara – The vicious cycle of existence wherein sentient beings create and perpetuate their own sufferings, lifetime after lifetime through their actions, speech and thoughts. Samsara consists of six realms of existence. This includes all beings in the hell realms, spirits, animals, humans, gods and demi-gods and crosses all dimensions of space and time.

Sangha – The community of monks and nuns. On a higher level this refers to the field of all enlightened Beings.

Sentient beings - All animate beings in samsara. Sentient beings refer not only to beings on our earth, but also on other planetary systems.

Sera (Monastery) – See Gaden

Setrap - a Dharma Protector who is an emanation of Buddha Amitabha. Setrap is the principal protector of Gaden Shartse monastery and Kechara House.

Shakyamuni – Lord Buddha, who 2,500 years ago set down the teachings that we continue to follow today.

Singdongma – The lion-faced dakini who provides protection from and elimination of very strong black magic or very negative energies.

Suffering - Suffering can be obvious such as in poverty, sickness, death, abuse, but also refers to our very subtle delusions that continually leave us dissatisfied with our lives. Suffering begins with our inherent grasping at an independent "I," which then leads to wrong projections that impermanent, material objects on the "outside" will bring us (the "I") happiness. When they disappoint us, we suffer.

Tara – The great female Buddha who emanates in 21 forms. Her most common form is Green Tara, representing Enlightened Activity and who is known for her swiftness in coming to our aid.

Tantra – The practice of taking the result onto the path where we identify with an Enlightened being instead of our limited personal concepts of ourselves. Tantra is practiced by the most advanced, sincere and committed practitioners.

Three Jewels – The Buddha, Dharma and Sangha.

Tsatsa – Small portable Buddha statues made from clay.

(Lama) Tsongkhapa – Also known as Je Rinpoche. One of Buddhism's most prominent masters of the 14th Century who was especially revered for his scholastic achievement and great teachings during his lifetime. He also founded the Gelug school of Buddhism and the great Gaden monastic tradition which has prevailed until today. Lama Tsongkhapa embodies three great Bodhisattvas at once – Avalokiteshvara, Manjushri, and Vajrapani – so praying to him is equivalent to calling upon these three Buddhas.

Vajrapani – Buddha of Spiritual Power.

Vajrasattva – Buddha of Purification.

Vajrayogini – A Buddha embodying the essence of wisdom and compassion, or bliss and Emptiness. She is one of the highest tantric deities, extremely relevant in our present time since her practice becomes more powerful as our delusions become stronger.

Yamantaka – A very wrathful emanation of Manjushri who can purify even the worst negative karma and protect against extremely harmful negative energies.

Yidam – A meditational deity (such as Tara, Manjushri, Lama Tsongkhapa) upon whom practitioners concentrate their practice to attain their respective Enlightened qualities.

Yogi(ni) – Somebody who has dedicated his/her life entirely to practice, usually in solitary retreat.

Appendix

Eight Verses of Transforming the mind
Kadampa Geshe Langri Tangpa, 1054-1123

With the determination to accomplish
The highest welfare for all sentient beings
Who surpass even a wish-fulfilling jewel
I will learn to hold them supremely dear.

Whenever I associate with others I will learn
To think of myself as the lowest of all
And respectfully hold others to be supreme
From the very depths of my heart.

In all actions I will learn to search into my mind
And as soon as an afflictive emotion arises
Endangering myself and others
I will firmly face and avert it.

I will learn to cherish all beings of bad nature
And those oppressed by strong sins and sufferings
As if I had found a precious
Treasure very difficult to find.

When others out of jealousy treat me badly
With abuse, slander and so on,
I will learn to take all loss
And offer the victory to them.

When one whom I have benefited with great hope
Unreasonably hurts me very badly,
I will learn to view that person
As an excellent spiritual guide.

In short, I will learn to offer to everyone without exception
All help and happiness directly and indirectly
And respectfully take upon myself
All harm and suffering of my mothers.

I will learn to keep all these practices
Undefiled by the stains of the eight worldly conceptions
And by understanding all phenomena as like illusions
Be released from the bondage of attachment.

Eight Worldly Conceptions
(also known as the Eight Worldly Concerns)

The concern to get:

1. Pleasure
2. Material Gain
3. Praise
4. Good reputation

The avoidance of:

5. Pain
6. Material Loss
7. Blame
8. Poor reputation

A PRAYER FOR BLESSINGS, PROSPERITY AND HOPE

I fold my hands to the Messenger of Peace
And Great Patron Saint of Tibet, **Lama Tsongkhapa**

I offer my Heart to the One who can bestow great calm of mind,
Avalokiteshvara, whom you embody, Lama Tsongkhapa

I offer my Speech to the One who can pacify inner and outer strife
Manjushri, whom you embody, Lama Tsongkhapa

I offer my Body to the One who can pacify negative inner/outer spirits
Vajrapani, whom you embody, Lama Tsongkhapa

In my Lord Lama Tsongkhapa, bless me to let go
of anger and revenge,

Bless me to control my speech which is the cause
of sufferings and happinesses,

I ask you to bless my body that it may be
used solely to benefit others.

Those who say this prayer remembering your holy qualities
– that you are no other but the embodiment of the three great Bodhisattvas.

May they and myself have our obstacles and unhappiness quelled.

By reciting your holy mantra may we gain uncommon siddhis,
realizations, may our temporal obstacles
be pacified and may we gain prosperity.

[Composed by Gaden Tsem Tulku, Tuesday 20th July, 2004 in Kuala Lumpur]

MIGTSEMA

Mig-Mey Tze-Wey Ter-Chen Chenrezig
Dri-Mey Khyen-Pi Wang-Po Jampal-Yang
Du-Pung Ma-Lu Jom-Dzey Sang-Wey Dag
Gang-Chen Ke-Pey Tsug-Gyen Tsongkhapa
Lo-Sang Trag-Pey Shab-La Sol-Wa Deb

Je Tsongkhapa, crown jewel of the Holy Masters
of the Land of Snows,
You are Avalokiteshvara, great goldmine of
compassion untainted by ego's delusion.
You are Manjushri, great master of stainless wisdom.
You are Vajrapani, great subduer of all the gatherings of demons.
At your feet, famed Lobsang Dragpa, I humbly bow and earnestly request
that all sentient beings achieve Enlightenment.

May His Holiness the Dalai Lama and all great Lamas have long life,
no obstacles to their Dharma work and be surrounded by
sound and enthusiastic students.

Kechara House, established in 2000, is a non-profit Tibetan Buddhist organisation under the spiritual direction of His Eminence Tsem Tulku Rinpoche. It is an affiliated branch of Gaden Shartse Monastery, which is now situated in Mundgod, South India. Gaden Shartse Monastery belongs to the Holy Gaden Monastery which now houses more than 3000 monks, and is one of the most elite monastic universities in the world.

The objective of Kechara House is to spread the beautiful teachings of Lord Buddha to as many people as possible, in the Southeast-Asian region and worldwide. It offers regular teachings from H.E. Tsem Tulku Rinpoche, and a range of programs ranging from introductory classes on Buddhism to regular prayer sessions. If you would like to know more about Kechara, please contact us through the following avenues :

1) **Kechara House**
   Unit 41-2A & 41-2B, 1st Floor,
   Jalan PJU 1/3C, SunwayMas Commercial Centre,
   47301 Petaling Jaya, Selangor, Malaysia
   Tel   : (+603) 7806 4582
   Fax   : (+603) 7804 5862
   E-mail   : kh_info@kechara.com
   Website : www.kecharahouse.com

2) **Personal website of H.E. Tsem Tulku Rinpoche** : www.tsemtulku.com
   This site contains Rinpoche's Dharma teachings, available online for downloads. It also contains background information on Rinpoche's life, our recent events as well as various publications.

3) Our **Kechara Dharma Outlets** specialise in Buddha statues and artifacts from Nepal and India, as well as aromatherapeutic products, Dharma books and Dharma CD/DVDs. Visit our website www.kechara.com to find our more!

Kechara Paradise
37B, 2nd Floor, Jalan SS2/75,
47300 Petaling Jaya,
Selangor, Malaysia
Tel : (+603) 7877 0071

Dzambala Mystical Treasures
S328F, 2nd Floor (New Wing),
One Utama Shopping Centre
No. 1, Lebuh Bandar Utama,
Bandar Utama Damansara,
47800 Petaling Jaya,
Selangor, Malaysia
Tel : (+603) 7710 4435

Kechara Mystical Treasures
F1.3, 1st Floor, Piccolo Galleria,
Jalan Bukit Bintang,
55100 Kuala Lumpur, Malaysia
Tel : (+603) 2148 0284

Yogini Mystical Treasures
P20B, 4th Floor,
Lot 10 Shopping Centre,
50 Jalan Sultan Ismail,
50250 Kuala Lumpur
Tel/Fax : (+603) 2144 2889